The Ultimate Real Estate Q&A

65 QUESTIONS EVERY HOMEBUYER MUST ASK

GLEEN WILLIAM

The Ultimate Real Estate Q&A: 65 Questions Every Homebuyer MUST Ask

Copyright © 2023 by Gleen William

All rights reserved. No part of this publication may be reproduced, distributed, or transmitted in any form or by any means, including photocopying, recording, or other electronic or mechanical methods, without the prior written permission of the publisher, except in the case of brief quotations embodied in critical reviews and certain other noncommercial uses permitted by copyright law.

This book is meant to provide broad knowledge and recommendations on the topic of real estate. It is not a substitute for professional guidance, and readers are encouraged to consult with trained professionals for specialized advice and help tailored to their specific circumstances. The author and publisher make no claims or warranties regarding the accuracy, completeness, or usefulness of the material provided herein and disclaim any liability for reliance on or use of this information.

The Ultimate Real Estate Q&A: 65 Questions Every Homebuyer MUST Ask

TABLE OF CONTENT

INTRODUCTION 7
WHAT ARE THE CURRENT TRENDS IN REAL ESTATE? 9
HOW DO I SET MY BUDGET FOR PURCHASING A HOME? 11
WHICH TYPE OF HOME LOAN IS BEST FOR ME? 13
HOW DO I IMPROVE MY CREDIT SCORE BEFORE BUYING? 15
WHAT SHOULD I LOOK FOR IN A NEIGHBORHOOD? 17
HOW DO I SELECT THE RIGHT REAL ESTATE AGENT? 19
WHAT DOCUMENTS SHOULD I PREPARE FOR THE PURCHASING PROCESS?...21
WHAT STEPS ARE INVOLVED IN THE HOME PURCHASING PROCESS?............23
HOW DO I KNOW IF A PROPERTY IS PRICED CORRECTLY?................25
WHAT FACTORS SHOULD I CONSIDER DURING A HOME INSPECTION? 27
HOW DO I KNOW IF A PROPERTY IS PRICED CORRECTLY?................29
WHAT IS ESCROW, AND HOW DOES IT WORK? 31
WHAT IS AN ESCROW OFFICER'S ROLE IN REAL ESTATE TRANSACTIONS? 33
WHAT IS A CONTINGENCY IN A REAL ESTATE CONTRACT?..............37
WHAT ARE CONTINGENCIES IN REAL ESTATE CONTRACTS? 39
WHAT ARE THE COMMON TYPES OF CONTINGENCIES IN REAL ESTATE CONTRACTS? 41
WHAT IS HOMEOWNER'S INSURANCE AND WHY IS IT IMPORTANT?............43
HOW DO I NEGOTIATE THE BEST DEAL WHEN PURCHASING A HOME?..........45
WHAT SHOULD I DO IF I HAVE PROBLEMS DURING THE HOMEBUYING PROCESS? 47
WHAT ARE COMMON MISTAKES TO AVOID WHEN PURCHASING A HOME?..49
WHAT IS A HOME WARRANTY, AND DO I NEED ONE? 51
WHAT'S THE DIFFERENCE BETWEEN A FIXED-RATE AND AN ADJUSTABLE-RATE MORTGAGE? 53

The Ultimate Real Estate Q&A: 65 Questions Every Homebuyer MUST Ask

WHAT ARE CLOSING COSTS, AND WHO PAYS FOR THEM?...........................55

WHAT IS PRIVATE MORTGAGE INSURANCE (PMI), AND DO I NEED IT?..........57

HOW DO I CHOOSE THE RIGHT NEIGHBORHOOD FOR BUYING A HOME? 59

HOW CAN I KNOW WHETHER I'M READY TO BUY A HOUSE?...........................61

WHAT IS EARNEST MONEY, AND HOW DOES IT WORK?......................................63

WHAT ARE HOME EQUITY LOANS AND LINES OF CREDIT (HELOCS)?.............65

HOW CAN I IMPROVE MY CREDIT SCORE PRIOR TO BUYING A HOME?..........67

WHAT IS A HOME APPRAISAL, AND WHY IS IT IMPORTANT?...........................69

WHAT ARE THE ADVANTAGES OF WORKING WITH A REAL ESTATE AGENT?..71

WHAT ARE HOME EQUITY LOANS AND LINES OF CREDIT (HELOCS)?.............73

HOW CAN I IMPROVE MY CREDIT SCORE PRIOR TO BUYING A HOME?..........75

WHAT IS A HOME APPRAISAL, AND WHY IS IT IMPORTANT?...........................77

WHAT ARE THE ADVANTAGES OF WORKING WITH A REAL ESTATE AGENT?..79

WHAT ARE SOME RED FLAGS TO LOOK OUT FOR WHEN BUYING A HOME?...81

HOW DOES THE HOME INSPECTION PROCESS WORK? 83

HOW DO PROPERTY TAXES WORK FOR HOMEOWNERS? 85

WHAT IS A SELLER'S DISCLOSURE, AND WHY IS IT IMPORTANT? 87

WHAT IS ESCROW, AND HOW DOES IT WORK IN REAL ESTATE? 89

WHAT IS A COUNTEROFFER IN REAL ESTATE? 91

WHAT IS A HOME WARRANTY AND SHOULD I BUY ONE?................................93

HOW DO PROPERTY TAXES WORK WHEN YOU BUY A HOME? 95

WHAT IS A CLOSING DISCLOSURE, AND WHY IS IT IMPORTANT?..................97

HOW DO I DETERMINE MY DEBT-TO-INCOME RATIO (DTI) FOR MORTGAGES? 99

WHAT ARE SOME TYPICAL CLOSING COSTS FOR BUYING A HOME?............101

WHAT IS PRIVATE MORTGAGE INSURANCE (PMI), AND DO I NEED IT?........103

The Ultimate Real Estate Q&A: 65 Questions Every Homebuyer MUST Ask

WHAT IS A HOME EQUITY LINE OF CREDIT (HELOC), AND HOW DOES IT WORK? 105

WHAT'S THE DISTINCTION BETWEEN A FIXED-RATE MORTGAGE AND AN ADJUSTABLE-RATE MORTGAGE (ARM)? 107

WHAT'S THE DIFFERENCE BETWEEN A CONVENTIONAL LOAN AND A GOVERNMENT-BACKED LOAN? 109

WHAT IS EARNEST MONEY, AND WHY IS IT IMPORTANT IN REAL ESTATE TRANSACTIONS? 111

WHAT IS A COMPARATIVE MARKET ANALYSIS (CMA), AND WHY IS IT USEFUL? 113

WHAT IS A HOMEOWNERS ASSOCIATION (HOA), AND WHAT ARE ITS RESPONSIBILITIES? 115

WHAT IS TITLE INSURANCE, AND WHY IS IT IMPORTANT? 117

WHAT IS A HOME INSPECTION, AND WHY IS IT IMPORTANT? 119

WHAT COMMON RED FLAGS SHOULD YOU LOOK FOR DURING A HOME INSPECTION? 121

WHAT IS AN ESCALATION CLAUSE IN A REAL ESTATE OFFER? 123

WHAT IS DUAL AGENCY IN REAL ESTATE? IS IT LEGAL? 125

WHAT IS A HOME WARRANTY, AND IS IT WORTH BUYING? 127

WHAT ARE SOME COMMON CLOSING COSTS IN REAL ESTATE TRANSACTIONS? 129

WHAT IS A HOME EQUITY LINE OF CREDIT (HELOC), AND HOW DOES IT WORK? 133

WHAT IS A LEASE OPTION IN REAL ESTATE, AND HOW DOES IT WORK? 135

WHAT IS PRIVATE MORTGAGE INSURANCE (PMI), AND WHEN IS IT REQUIRED? 137

WHAT IS A 1031 EXCHANGE IN REAL ESTATE INVESTING? 139

WHAT IS A REVERSE MORTGAGE, AND HOW DOES IT WORK? 143

WHAT IS A SHORT SALE IN REAL ESTATE, AND HOW DOES IT WORK? 147

The Ultimate Real Estate Q&A: 65 Questions Every Homebuyer MUST Ask

WHAT ARE THE HIDDEN COSTS OF HOMEOWNERSHIP? 151

WHAT ARE SOME IMPORTANT CONSIDERATIONS WHEN INVESTING IN RENTAL PROPERTIES? 153

WHAT ARE SOME TIPS FOR NEGOTIATING A HOME PURCHASE PRICE? 157

CONCLUSION 161

ACKNOWLEDGMENT 163

INTRODUCTION

Welcome to "The Ultimate Real Estate Q&A: 65 Questions Every Homebuyer MUST Ask," your comprehensive guide to navigating the fascinating world of real estate with confidence and clarity. Whether you're a first-time homebuyer entering the market for the first time or a seasoned investor trying to diversify your portfolio, this book contains vital insights, practical advice, and professional suggestions to help you make informed decisions at every stage.

Imagine you're standing on the threshold of your dream home, holding the keys to your future. But how did you arrive here? The path to homeownership is full of twists and turns, from obtaining the necessary finance to discovering the ideal property and negotiating a reasonable price. That's where "The Ultimate Real Estate Q&A" comes in, as your dependable companion on this exciting trip.

In the following pages, you'll find answers to sixty-five important questions that every homebuyer should ask, covering a wide range of themes critical to your success in the real estate market. We'll start by demystifying mortgages, going over several loan alternatives, and explaining the intricacies of interest rates, down payments, and closing expenses.

But that's only the beginning. As we progress through the book, you'll learn important information about property inspections, title insurance, escrow procedures, and other topics. We'll answer challenging questions on negotiating purchase prices, managing short sales and foreclosures, and even looking into alternative investment strategies like 1031 exchanges and reverse mortgages.

Each chapter focuses on a separate aspect of the home-buying process, providing clear, succinct answers to common queries as well as practical guidance and real-world examples to help clarify crucial concepts. Along the way, you'll discover useful ideas, professional insights, and actionable methods to aid you on this fascinating journey.

But here's the best part: at the end of each chapter, we'll leave you with a teaser—a tempting view into the next topic on the horizon that will make you want to turn the page and discover even more useful ideas. Whether it's deciphering the complexities of private mortgage insurance, navigating leasing choices, or mastering the art of negotiating a home purchase price, each chapter builds on the previous one, bringing you closer to your dream of homeownership.

So, are you prepared to begin on this trip with us? Whether you're a first-time buyer or a seasoned pro, "The Ultimate Real Estate Q&A" is your guide to success in the ever-changing real estate market. Let's dive in and find the keys to realizing your homeownership aspirations together!

WHAT ARE THE CURRENT TRENDS IN REAL ESTATE?

Hello there, potential homeowner! Are you prepared to embark on the exciting process of purchasing your dream home? Before you enter into the realm of real estate, let's talk about something very important: market trends. Yes, it is right! Understanding the real estate market can significantly improve your home-buying experience.

So, what really constitutes market trends? Simply expressed, these are the trends and shifts in the housing market that can influence anything from property prices to inventory levels. And believe me, staying current with these trends can give you a significant advantage when it comes to selecting the ideal home.

Let's break it down a little more. You'll want to know if it's a buyer's or seller's market. In a buyer's market, there are more properties for sale than buyers, which may give you an advantage when negotiating rates. In contrast, in a seller's market, there are more buyers than available homes, resulting in heightened competition and potentially higher prices.

But wait—there's more! Interest rates and property affordability are also important factors to consider.

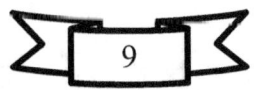

Low interest rates make borrowing money for a mortgage more inexpensive, whilst high interest rates have the reverse impact. Of course, house affordability plays a significant role in assessing if now is a good time to buy.

Now, let me give you a real-life example to illustrate this idea. Assume you're looking for a property in a community where prices have been steadily rising over the last few months. This could indicate that it is now a seller's market, and you will need to act quickly if you locate a home you want. On the other hand, if you're in a market where prices have been falling and there's a lot of inventory to pick from, you may have more leeway to haggle and take your time locating the ideal property.

So, how can you keep up with all of these industry trends? Fortunately, there are several services available to assist you. You can monitor local real estate websites, read the most recent news items, or speak with a reputable real estate agent who understands the market.

The following chapter discussed how to set a budget for buying a property. Trust me, you won't want to miss it!

HOW DO I SET MY BUDGET FOR PURCHASING A HOME?

Okay, let's get into the nitty gritty of home buying: your budget! Calculating how much you can comfortably spend on your new home is critical. But don't worry, I'm here to explain it down for you in simple terms.

First and foremost, assess your financial situation. How much do you make per month? And how much do you spend on bills, groceries, and, let's be honest, the occasional indulgence in your favorite guilty pleasures? It's critical to have a clear picture of your monthly income and expenses so you can determine how much you have left over for housing costs.

Next, let's discuss debt. Are there any outstanding debts or credit card balances? If so, include those in your budget as well. Lenders will consider your debt-to-income ratio when considering how much they are ready to offer you, so you should be aware of where you stand.

Now for the exciting part: saving for a down payment. Most lenders will demand you to put down a specific proportion of the home's buying price up front. The standard is usually approximately 20%, however there are programs for first-time homebuyers that allow for smaller down payments. Remember that the more you can put down upfront, the lower your monthly mortgage payments will be.

But wait—there's more to consider! You should also consider additional expenses such as property taxes, homeowners' insurance, and upkeep charges. These can add up quickly, so incorporate them into your budget from the start.

Now, let me provide a real-life example to demonstrate this notion. Let's imagine you make $5,000 per month after taxes and have $2,000 in monthly costs. That leaves you roughly $3,000 each month to cover housing expenses. If you want to make a 20% down payment on a $300,000 home, you'll need $60,000 up front. You'll also need to budget for property taxes, insurance, and upkeep, which might add a few hundred dollars to your monthly spending.

So, how do you put it all together to create your budget? It's similar to piecing together a puzzle. You'll need to carefully analyze all of the components - your income, expenses, savings, and additional charges - and fit them together to obtain a sense of what you can actually afford.

In the next chapter: We'll go over the various types of house loans available and help you determine which is ideal for your budget and financial circumstances. Trust me, you won't want to miss it!

WHICH TYPE OF HOME LOAN IS BEST FOR ME?

Okay, let's talk about home loans! With so many alternatives available, deciding which one is best for you might be difficult. But don't worry, I'll explain everything so you can make an informed decision.

First, let's discuss the most prevalent sort of home loan: the conventional loan. This is your standard mortgage that is not backed by any government body. Conventional loans normally need a 20% down payment and tight credit score criteria, but they can provide lower interest rates and greater flexibility in loan arrangements.

Next, we have FHA loans. These are Federal Housing Administration-backed loans that are popular among first-time homebuyers who do not have a big down payment. An FHA loan allows you to put down as little as 3.5% and may qualify with a lower credit score than a conventional loan. However, FHA loans require additional mortgage insurance premiums, which might increase your monthly payments.

Then there are VA loans, which are designed particularly for active-duty military personnel, veterans, and qualifying surviving spouses. VA loans provide 100% financing with no down payment and typically have lower interest rates than conventional loans. Furthermore, they do not require private mortgage insurance, which may save you money in the long term.

Don't forget about USDA loans, which are intended for low- to moderate-income borrowers in rural communities. These loans provide 100% financing with no down payment and often have interest rates that are lower than the market. However, eligibility is subject to rigorous income and geography limitations.

Now, let me provide a real-life example to demonstrate this notion. Assume you're a first-time homebuyer with little savings for a down payment. An FHA loan may be a suitable fit for you because it provides for a lower down payment and more flexible credit score requirements. On the other hand, if you are a veteran trying to buy a home with no money down, a VA loan may be the way to go.

So, how can you choose which form of home loan is right for you? It all boils down to your personal financial condition and ambitions. Take your time weighing the pros and disadvantages of each option, and don't be hesitant to talk with a reputable lender who can point you in the proper direction.

In the next chapter: We'll discuss how to raise your credit score before purchasing a home so that you may qualify for the best loan conditions possible. Trust me, you won't want to miss it!

HOW DO I IMPROVE MY CREDIT SCORE BEFORE BUYING?

Okay, let's talk about a critical component of the homebuying process: your credit score. Your credit score is a crucial factor in determining whether you qualify for a mortgage and what interest rate you are offered. But don't panic, there are plenty of things you can take to improve your credit score before becoming a homeowner.

First and foremost, examine your credit record. Every year, you can request a free copy of your credit report from each of the three major credit bureaus: Equifax, Experian, and TransUnion. Reviewing your credit report can offer you a clear picture of where you are and allow you to identify any problems or inaccuracies that may be lowering your score.

Next, concentrate on paying off your current debt. Your credit usage ratio, which compares the amount of credit you use to your total available credit, is an important element in determining your credit score. Keep your credit use below 30% to demonstrate good credit management.

If you have any delinquent accounts or collections on your credit record, attempt to rectify them. Paying off past-due amounts or negotiating settlements with creditors might help boost your credit score over time.

Don't forget about the annoying late payments! Payment history is the single most essential component in determining your credit score, so always pay your payments on time. Set up automatic payments or reminders to keep you on track and prevent repeat mistakes.

Now, let me give you a real-life example to illustrate this idea. Assume you have a credit card with a $1,000 limit and a $500 balance. That suggests your credit utilization percentage is 50%, which may be lowering your score. By paying down your balance to $300, you can reduce your utilization ratio to 30% and potentially improve your credit score.

So, how long will it take to observe improvement in your credit score? It relies on your own financial status and the efforts you take to remedy any problems. Overall, you may anticipate to see incremental improvements over time as you demonstrate appropriate credit management.

Here's a short tip for the next chapter: We'll discuss things to look for in a community when purchasing a home so you can locate the ideal area to settle down. Trust me, you won't want to miss it!

WHAT SHOULD I LOOK FOR IN A NEIGHBORHOOD?

Hello there, potential neighbor! Before you start planning where to display your favorite artwork or how to arrange your furniture, consider something as important: the neighborhood. After all, selecting the ideal community can make or break your home-buying journey. So, what should you look for?

First, let's discuss safety. You will want to feel safe in your new community, so examine crime rates and safety statistics. Seek out neighborhoods with low crime rates and a strong sense of community. Drive around at different times of day and night to get a sense of the area's character and ensure you feel safe going around.

Next, let's talk about amenities. What's nearby that matters to you? Are you a foodie who enjoys exploring new restaurants? Do you prefer spending time outside in parks or recreational areas? Perhaps you are seeking for reputable schools for your children or convenient access to public transit. Make a list of must-have amenities and rank the communities that tick the most boxes.

But wait—there's more! Let's discuss property values. While you're looking for the right property, you should also evaluate the neighborhood's long-term investment possibilities.

Look for regions where property values have gradually risen over time, since this may signal a desirable and stable community.

Now, let me provide a real-life example to demonstrate this notion. Assume you're a young professional who enjoys the hustle and bustle of city life. You value walkability and proximity to fashionable eateries and nightclubs. You might wish to narrow your search to up-and-coming urban neighborhoods that have a lively ambiance and plenty of facilities within walking distance.

So, how can you choose the best neighborhood for you? It's all about doing your homework and taking the time to investigate various topics. Talk to locals, read online neighborhood reviews, and go for walks in the region to get a sense of the community. Also, don't be hesitant to trust your gut instinct; if something doesn't seem right, it's probably not the ideal fit for you.

Nevertheless, in the next chapter: We'll go over how to select the best real estate agent to help you navigate the home-buying process with ease. Trust me, you won't want to miss it!

HOW DO I SELECT THE RIGHT REAL ESTATE AGENT?

Okay, now it's time to talk about your real estate agent, who will be your trusted guide through the twists and turns of the homebuying process. But, with so many agents available, how can you choose the best one for you? Let us break it down into simple steps.

First and foremost, you should conduct your own research. Begin by asking friends, family, and colleagues for recommendations. Personal references are frequently the most effective way to identify a reliable agent with a track record of success. You may also read internet reviews and visit agents' websites to get a sense of their skills and experience.

The next step is to conduct interviews with possible agents. Treat it like a job interview; after all, you're employing them to assist you with one of your most important financial decisions! Inquire about their experience in the local market, bargaining abilities, and attitude to client communication. You'll want to discover someone who is attentive to your demands and has your best interests in mind.

But don't take their word for it; ask for references. A reputable agent should be happy to give you with contact information for previous clients who can attest to their professionalism and efficacy. Contact these references and inquire about their experience working with the agent.

Now, let me provide a real-life example to demonstrate this notion. Assume you're a first-time homebuyer who is feeling a touch overwhelmed by the entire process. You want an agent that will gently guide you through each stage and explain everything in plain English. During your interviews, you discover an agent who not only has years of expertise, but also has a talent for simplifying complex concepts. Bingo, you've found your perfect mate!

So, how can you know whether you have discovered the proper agent? It's similar to discovering the ideal pair of shoes: you just know. Trust your instincts and find an agent who makes you feel secure and comfortable.

WHAT DOCUMENTS SHOULD I PREPARE FOR THE PURCHASING PROCESS?

Alright, brace up because we're about to get into the paperwork! When it comes to buying a home, you'll need to have everything in order, including the necessary documentation. Let us boil it down into simple terms.

First, gather your financial paperwork. This includes pay stubs, W-2s, and tax returns from the previous few years. Your lender will examine these documents to verify your income and determine whether you are financially secure enough to qualify for a mortgage.

Let us now discuss proof of assets. This may include bank statements, investment account statements, and evidence for any other assets you own. Your lender will want to verify that you have enough money set up for a down payment and closing costs, so be prepared to submit proof for all of your assets.

But wait—there's more! You will also need to obtain documentation regarding your work and residency. This could contain employment verification letters, tenancy agreements, and utility bills. Your lender will want to see that you have a steady work and a track record of paying your expenses on time.

Now, let me provide a real-life example to demonstrate this notion. Let's imagine you're a young professional who has been renting an apartment for several years. You will need to compile your pay stubs to confirm your income, as well as your rental agreement to demonstrate your history of timely payments. You will also be required to submit paperwork for any savings or assets used to meet the down payment and closing charges.

So, how do you keep organized during the document gathering process? It's all about making a checklist and staying on top of deadlines. Begin collecting your paperwork early in the home-buying process and keep them arranged in a file or folder. That way, if your lender requests something, you'll be prepared to offer it without any last-minute scrambling.

WHAT STEPS ARE INVOLVED IN THE HOME PURCHASING PROCESS?

Okay, let's take it step by step: the home buying procedure. It may appear intimidating at first, but believe me, it isn't as complicated as it sounds. Here's a simplified version to walk you through:

Get Pre-Approved for a Mortgage: Before you begin house looking, you need know how much you can afford. Getting pre-approved for a mortgage will help you understand your budget and show sellers that you are a serious buyer.

Find the Right Real Estate Agent: Your real estate agent will guide you through the entire process, from finding properties to negotiating the sale. Take your time in finding an agent that knows your requirements and has experience in your target area.

Begin house hunting: This is the exciting phase! Your agent will assist you in finding properties that suit your requirements and scheduling showings for you to attend. Don't be hesitant to ask questions and spend time examining each home.

Make an Offer: Once you've discovered the ideal location, it's time to submit an offer. Your agent will assist you in determining a reasonable price and negotiating with the seller on your behalf.

Home examination: A professional home examination is required prior to closing the transaction. This will reveal any potential faults with the property that you may have overlooked during your initial visit.

Secure Financing: Once your offer has been approved, you must finalize your mortgage financing. Work together with your lender to supply any additional documentation required and complete the underwriting process.

Closing: Now it's time to seal the deal! This is when you will sign all of the paperwork, pay any outstanding closing expenses, and formally assume ownership of the property. Congratulations, you are now a homeowner!

HOW DO I KNOW IF A PROPERTY IS PRICED CORRECTLY?

Ah, the age-old question: is this house worth its price? Determining whether a house is priced correctly needs some detective work, but don't worry, I have you covered. Here are some crucial points to consider:

Comparable Sales: Examine recent sales of comparable houses in the neighborhood to get a sense of what similar homes are selling for. This will provide you with a baseline for comparison and allow you to decide whether the asking price is consistent with market trends.

Consider the property's condition and any upgrades or renovations that have been completed. A well-maintained property with modern facilities may justify a higher asking price, whereas a fixer-upper may support a lower offer.

Location, Location, Location: A property's value is heavily influenced by its location. School districts, proximity to facilities, and neighborhood desirability all have an impact on price.

Market Conditions: Think about the status of the real estate market. In a seller's market, where demand exceeds supply, prices may rise. In a buyer's market, where supply exceeds demand, prices may be reduced.

Appraisal: After you make an offer on a home, your lender will request an appraisal to assess its market value. If the appraisal is lower than the agreed-upon purchase price, you may need to renegotiate with the seller or walk away from the transaction.

By taking these aspects into account and working closely with your real estate agent, you will be better able to decide whether a home is reasonably priced and make an informed decision about whether to make an offer.

WHAT FACTORS SHOULD I CONSIDER DURING A HOME INSPECTION?

All right, future homeowner, let us roll up our sleeves and get down to business: home inspections. This phase is critical in ensuring that the home you are looking at is in excellent condition and free of any hidden surprises. So, what should you look for during your home inspection? Let us break it down:

Structural Integrity: The inspector will carefully evaluate the home's structure, including the foundation, walls, roof, and attic, to ensure that everything is sound and free of severe problems such as cracks or water damage.

Plumbing: They will also inspect the plumbing system, which includes pipes, fixtures, and drains, to ensure that everything is in working condition and free of leaks or obstructions.

Electrical Systems: The inspector will examine the electrical system to ensure that it complies with current safety requirements and is free of hazards such as defective wiring or overloaded circuits.

HVAC Systems: They will inspect the heating, ventilation, and air conditioning (HVAC) systems to ensure that they are operational and efficient. This involves inspecting the furnace, air conditioner, and ductwork for any concerns.

Appliances and Fixtures: The inspector will test all the home's appliances and fixtures, including the stove, dishwasher, and faucets, to confirm they are in working order. They will also look for evidence of damage or wear and tear.

Pest and Mold Infestations: They will check the house for evidence of pest infestations, such as termites or rats, as well as mold or mildew growth, which might signal moisture problems.

Finally, the inspector will look for any potential safety issues in the home, such as missing stair railings, defective smoke alarms, or hazardous electrical outlets.

Once the inspection is completed, you will receive a thorough report explaining any faults discovered. This information will assist you in making an informed decision about whether to proceed with the purchase, negotiate repairs with the seller, or walk away from the transaction entirely.

Remember, a home inspection is your chance to discover any potential problems with the property before you commit to purchasing it. So, do not neglect this step; it could save you a lot of time, money, and hassles eventually.

HOW DO I KNOW IF A PROPERTY IS PRICED CORRECTLY?

Hello there, clever homebuyer! Are you ready to handle one of real estate's most essential questions? Let us chat about prices. Knowing whether a property is reasonably priced can save you a significant amount of time, money, and stress during the home-buying process. Here is how to determine if a property's pricing is reasonable:

Comparative Market Analysis (CMA): Examine recent sales data for comparable houses in the neighborhood. A CMA will provide you a clear picture of what similar houses have recently sold for, allowing you to determine whether the asking price is in line with market trends.

Consider the condition of the property. Is it move-in ready, or does it require substantial repairs and updates? Adjust your price evaluation depending on the property's condition in comparison to comparable properties in the neighborhood.

Location Factors: Location is important! Consider community amenities, school districts, proximity to transportation, and other factors that influence property values. A prime location may justify a premium price.

Market Conditions: Determine the present situation of the real estate market. In a seller's market with high demand and low inventory, prices may rise. Prices may be more negotiable in a buyer's market, if supply exceeds demand.

Appraisal Value: When you make an offer on a property, your lender will order an appraisal to determine its value. If the appraisal is lower than the agreed-upon purchase price, it may suggest that the property is overpriced.

By taking these aspects into account and working closely with your real estate agent, you will be better able to decide whether a property's price is reasonable for its current market value.

WHAT IS ESCROW, AND HOW DOES IT WORK?

Escrow may sound like a sophisticated term, but it is essentially a simple notion that plays an important part in the home-purchase process. Let us break it out in simple terms.

What is Escrow? It is a neutral third-party account that holds funds during the home-buying process. It acts as a liaison between the buyer and seller, ensuring that both parties meet their commitments before the transaction is completed.

How Does It Work?: When you make an offer on a home and the seller accepts it, you normally deposit earnest money into escrow. This notifies the seller that you are serious about purchasing the home. The monies are held in escrow until closing, at which time they are applied to your down payment and closing costs.

The escrow officer is often a professional from a title or escrow business who handles the escrow process. They will check that all required documentation and finances are in order before the transaction is completed.

Timeline: The timeline for the escrow process varies dependent on factors such as transaction complexity and lender criteria. Escrow typically opens as soon as the purchase agreement is completed and remains open until the closing.

conditions: During the escrow period, both the buyer and seller may be required to meet specific conditions mentioned in the purchase agreement. These could involve completing a home inspection, appraisal, or obtaining financing approval.

Closing: After all contingencies have been met and the lender has financed the loan, the deal enters the closing stage. At closing, the leftover money is deposited in escrow, and the escrow officer distributes them to the proper parties, such as the seller, real estate agents, and any other parties engaged in the transaction.

Overall, escrow is a safe and effective way to handle the financial parts of a real estate transaction, offering buyers and sellers peace of mind throughout.

WHAT IS AN ESCROW OFFICER'S ROLE IN REAL ESTATE TRANSACTIONS?

An escrow officer is responsible for arranging the closing of a real estate transaction. The following is an overview of an escrow officer's responsibilities and duties:

The escrow officer serves as a neutral middleman between the buyer, seller, lender, and other parties to the transaction. The escrow officer keeps critical documents and monies in escrow until all the sale conditions are completed and the transaction is ready to close.

Opening Escrow: Once the buyer and seller have signed a purchase agreement, the escrow officer opens an escrow account to keep the earnest money deposit and other transaction cash.

The escrow officer gathers appropriate documents and information from the parties involved and ensures that all required documentation is completed and signed.

Title Search and Examination: The escrow officer collaborates with a title company to conduct a title search and examination of the property to ensure that there are no liens, encumbrances, or legal concerns that could jeopardize the transaction. The escrow officer checks the title commitment and addresses any title concerns that may emerge prior to closing.

The escrow officer works with the buyer, seller, lender, real estate agents, and other parties to schedule the closing date and time. The escrow officer creates the closing documents, which include the settlement statement, deed, and other legal documents required for the transaction.

monies Disbursement: At closing, the escrow officer uses monies from the escrow account to pay off the seller's existing mortgage, closing charges, and any other transaction-related expenses. The escrow officer ensures that the money is distributed correctly and in compliance with the purchase agreement and closing instructions.

Document Recording: Following the closing, the escrow officer arranges for the deed and other legal documents to be recorded at the proper county or municipal office. Recording ensures that the transfer of ownership is formally documented and entered into the public records.

Communication and Customer Service: During the escrow procedure, the escrow officer acts as a liaison between the buyer, seller, and other parties involved in the transaction. The escrow officer gives updates and information on the transaction's status, as well as answers any queries or concerns.

Compliance and Legal Requirements: The escrow officer ensures that the transaction follows all applicable laws, regulations, and contractual responsibilities. The escrow officer adheres to industry best practices and ethical standards to protect the interests of all parties engaged in the transaction.

Overall, the escrow officer is crucial to the successful and efficient closing of a real estate transaction. By acting as a neutral middleman, managing the closing process, and ensuring legal and regulatory compliance, the escrow officer contributes to a smooth and successful closing experience for purchasers, sellers, and lenders.

WHAT IS A CONTINGENCY IN A REAL ESTATE CONTRACT?

A contingency is a condition or requirement that must be met before a real estate contract is considered binding and enforceable. Contingencies safeguard buyers by allowing them to terminate the contract without penalty if specific requirements are not met. Here are some typical contingencies included in real estate contracts:

A financing contingency permits the buyer to cancel the contract if they are unable to obtain financing for the purchase of the property. If the buyer is unable to acquire a mortgage loan within the stated timeframe, they may cancel the contract and receive a refund of their earnest money deposit.

A home inspection contingency permits the buyer to perform a professional house examination on the property. If the inspection reveals substantial faults or defects that the buyer refuses to accept, they may request repairs, credits, or renegotiate the terms of the contract. If an agreement cannot be reached, the buyer may choose to withdraw from the contract.

Appraisal Contingency: If the property appraises for less than the agreed-upon purchase price, the buyer may withdraw from the contract.

If the property appraises for less than the purchase price, the buyer may request that the seller drop the price to reflect the evaluated value or give additional monies to cover the deficit.

A sale contingency allows the buyer to withdraw from the contract if they are unable to sell their current house within a set time limit. This condition is frequent among buyers who must sell their current house before purchasing a new one.

A title contingency permits the buyer to terminate the contract if any title flaws or difficulties are identified during the title search procedure. If the title search reveals liens, encumbrances, or other difficulties that impact the property's ownership rights, the buyer may have the right to cancel the contract.

Contingencies allow buyers to undertake due diligence and defend their interests before completing the acquisition of a property. Buyers must carefully research and understand the contingencies specified in the contract, as well as consult with their real estate agent or attorney, to ensure that their interests are effectively safeguarded.

WHAT ARE CONTINGENCIES IN REAL ESTATE CONTRACTS?

Contingencies are stipulations in a real estate contract that specify which conditions or events must occur for the contract to be binding. Here are some typical contingencies included in real estate contracts:

A financial contingency allows the buyer to exit the contract if they are unable to obtain financing for the acquisition. It usually describes the sort of finance the buyer expects to receive and the date for obtaining a loan commitment.

An appraisal contingency gives the buyer the option to cancel the contract or renegotiate the purchase price if the property appraises for less than the agreed-upon price. It helps the buyer avoid overpaying for the property.

A home inspection contingency permits the buyer to perform a professional house inspection and then negotiate repairs or credits with the seller based on the results. If substantial flaws are discovered during the inspection, the buyer may have the right to cancel the contract.

A sale contingency allows the buyer to cancel the contract if they are unable to sell their current house within a certain timeframe.

This contingency is frequent among buyers who must sell their current house in order to finance the purchase of a new one.

A title contingency allows the buyer to cancel the contract if any issues with the title, such as liens, encroachments, or easements, are not resolved to their satisfaction.

A home sale contingency allows the buyer to cancel the contract if they are unable to sell their current home within a certain time period. This contingency is frequent among buyers who must sell their current house in order to finance the purchase of a new one.

Contingencies protect buyers by allowing them to cancel the contract if specific conditions are not met or unforeseen concerns develop during the due diligence process. They allow buyers to proceed with confidence, knowing that if things do not go as planned, they have an exit strategy.

WHAT ARE THE COMMON TYPES OF CONTINGENCIES IN REAL ESTATE CONTRACTS?

Contingencies may sound like a fancy legal phrase, but they are a valuable safety net for both buyers and sellers in a real estate transaction. Let us break it out in simple terms.

What Are Contingencies?: Contingencies are requirements that must be completed before a real estate transaction may proceed. They safeguard both the buyer and the seller by allowing either party to cancel the contract if specified requirements are not satisfied.

Types of Contingencies: Common contingencies are:

Home Inspection Contingency: This permits the buyer to have the property inspected by an expert, negotiate repairs, or withdraw from the contract if substantial faults are discovered.

Appraisal Contingency: This guarantees that the property will appraise for at least the purchase amount. If the appraisal comes in lower, the buyer has the option to renegotiate the price or cancel the contract.

Financing contingency: This allows the buyer time to acquire financing for the acquisition. If they are unable to get a mortgage by the given period, they may cancel the arrangement without penalty.

Sale Contingency: This permits the buyer to make the purchase contingent on selling their existing house. If they are unable to sell their house within a defined timeframe, they have the option to cancel the contract.

Negotiation: Contingencies are frequently negotiated between the buyer and seller. For example, the seller may offer to fix specific repairs found during the inspection in exchange for the buyer waiving the appraisal contingency.

Timeline: The purchase agreement usually specifies the deadlines for contingent liabilities. Both parties must meet these dates in order for the transaction to proceed smoothly.

Overall, contingencies give safety and flexibility for both buyers and sellers in a real estate transaction, allowing them to move forward with confidence knowing that their interests are protected.

WHAT IS HOMEOWNER'S INSURANCE AND WHY IS IT IMPORTANT?

Homeowners insurance may not be the most thrilling purchase, but it is an essential component of preserving your investment in your house. In a nutshell, here's why it matters:

Homeowners insurance protects you financially in the event that your house is damaged or destroyed by a covered risk such as fire, theft, vandalism, or natural disaster. It contributes to the expense of repairing or rebuilding your home, allowing you to get back on your feet.

Liability Coverage: In addition to insuring your house, homeowners' insurance includes liability coverage. This can help pay legal and medical expenses if someone is hurt on your property and you are found to be at fault.

Mortgage Requirement: If you have a mortgage on your house, your lender will most likely need you to obtain homeowners insurance to protect their investment. Even if you own your house fully, it's always a good idea to protect yourself financially.

Peace of Mind: There are risks associated with home ownership, ranging from robbery to natural calamities.

Having homeowners' insurance provides you with peace of mind, knowing that you are financially covered against unexpected disasters.

Additional Coverage Options: Depending on your requirements, you can supplement your homes insurance policy with flood insurance, earthquake insurance, or personal property coverage for expensive goods such as jewelry or artwork.

Affordability: Homeowners insurance is often affordable; especially given the degree of protection it provides. The cost of your policy will be determined by criteria such as your home's worth, location, and the coverage options you select.

Overall, homeowners' insurance is an important investment that gives financial security and peace of mind to you and your family. It's a little sum to pay for the peace of mind that comes with knowing your home is insured in the case of an unexpected disaster.

HOW DO I NEGOTIATE THE BEST DEAL WHEN PURCHASING A HOME?

Negotiating the best deal when purchasing a home is a skill that may save you money and ensure you get the most bang for your buck. Here are some techniques for negotiating like a pro:

Do Your Research: In the realm of negotiation, knowledge is power. Investigate comparable sales in the region to get an idea of how much similar properties have sold for recently. This will provide you with a benchmark for what is considered a fair price for the home you are interested in.

Know Your Priorities: Before you start negotiating, make a list of your property priorities and requirements. Are you prepared to spend more for a home with newer kitchen appliances or a larger backyard? Knowing your priorities will help you focus your negotiations on what is most important to you.

Be Willing to Walk Away: One of the most effective negotiation strategies is to be prepared to walk away if the terms aren't beneficial to you.

This provides you leverage and shows the seller that you're serious about receiving a fair deal.

Don't Tip Your Hand: Keep your cards close to your chest when negotiating. Avoid exposing your maximum budget or how much you adore the home, since this can weaken your position and offer the seller an advantage.

Negotiate More Than Just money: While money is crucial, other components of the transaction can be bargained as well. Consider bargaining for seller-paid closing fees, property repairs or renovations, or a faster closing date.

Work with a Skilled Real Estate Agent: A skilled real estate agent might be your most valuable ally during negotiations. They understand the bargaining process and can advocate on your behalf to assist you receive the best possible price.

Be Respectful and Professional: Keep a respectful and professional manner during the negotiation process. Building rapport with both the seller and their agent can help you reach a mutually advantageous deal.

By following these suggestions and methods, you can improve your chances of getting the greatest deal while purchasing a home. With careful planning and a little insight, you'll be well on your way to purchasing your dream home at the appropriate price.

WHAT SHOULD I DO IF I HAVE PROBLEMS DURING THE HOMEBUYING PROCESS?

Problems arise during the homebuying process; however, understanding how to deal with them can help reduce stress and assure a good end. Here's what to do if you run across problems:

Stay Calm and Communicate: The first step is to remain calm and maintain open lines of communication with all parties involved, including your real estate agent, lender, and seller's agent. Any problems or issues you have should be clearly communicated so that they can be handled as soon as possible.

Consult Your Real Estate Agent: Your real estate agent is your advocate throughout the home-buying process and may provide advice and support if problems arise. Lean on their knowledge and experience to assist you handle any problems that emerge.

Review your contract: Examine your purchase agreement and any contingencies stated therein. If the problem is caused by the seller failing to meet a contingency or breaching the contract, you may have recourse.

Seek Legal Advice if Necessary: If the problem is serious or you are unsure about your rights and duties, consult a real estate attorney. They can offer legal advice and protect your interests during the procedure.

Consider Your possibilities: Depending on the nature of the issue, you may have several possibilities for resolution. This could involve renegotiating the terms of the contract, asking repairs or credits from the seller, or, in extreme situations, walking away from the transaction entirely.

Document everything. Keep careful records of all interactions, agreements, and issues encountered during the home-buying process. This documentation may be useful if you need to escalate the situation or take legal action.

Stay Flexible: Be willing to compromise and be adaptable in order to reach a solution. Sometimes finding a mutually acceptable solution necessitates that both parties yield a little.

Remember that troubles during the homebuying process are not unusual, and how you approach them will ultimately determine the outcome. You can successfully finish your house purchase by being calm, speaking properly, and requesting support as needed.

WHAT ARE COMMON MISTAKES TO AVOID WHEN PURCHASING A HOME?

Purchasing a home is a major choice, and it is critical to avoid common traps that might derail your home-buying experience. Here are some mistakes you should avoid:

Skipping Pre-Approval: Ignoring the pre-approval process can be a huge error. Getting pre-approved for a mortgage allows you to better understand your budget and demonstrates to sellers that you are a serious buyer.

Failure to Budget for Hidden charges: Don't overlook hidden charges such as closing costs, property taxes, homeowners insurance, and maintenance costs. Failure to budget for these expenses can cause financial difficulties in the future.

Skipping the Home Inspection: Skipping the home inspection to save money or time is a risky decision. A comprehensive assessment can reveal hidden flaws with the property, potentially costing you thousands of dollars in future repairs.

Ignoring Location: They say that location is everything in real estate, and this is true! Don't underestimate the significance of location when purchasing a home. Consider things like closeness to amenities, school districts, and travel time.

Maxing Out Your Budget: Just because you've been accepted for a specific loan amount does not mean you should spend it all. Be realistic about your budget and provide some wiggle room for unanticipated expenses.

Not shopping around for mortgage rates. Failing to look around for the best mortgage rates might cost you thousands of dollars over the course of your loan. Take the time to compare rates from other lenders to ensure you are getting the greatest price.

Not Working with a Real Estate Agent: Attempting to navigate the homebuying process on your own might be daunting. Working with a knowledgeable real estate agent will help you avoid typical pitfalls and ensure a more seamless transaction.

Avoiding these frequent pitfalls and working with a competent team of specialists will help you have a successful and stress-free homebuying experience.

WHAT IS A HOME WARRANTY, AND DO I NEED ONE?

A home warranty is a service contract that covers the repair or replacement of major household equipment and appliances. A house warranty, while not necessary, can provide homeowners with peace of mind and financial security. Here's what you should know.

Coverage: Home warranties often include coverage for HVAC, plumbing, electrical, and major appliances such as refrigerators, dishwashers, and ovens. Some warranties may also include optional coverage for pool equipment and garage door openers.

Cost: The price of a home warranty varies depending on the level of coverage, the size of your property, and the provider. Typically, the annual premium ranges from a few hundred to a thousand dollars.

Service Calls: If a covered system or appliance fails, you will notify the warranty provider and file a claim. They will arrange for a service technician to come out and assess the problem. Each service call will normally incur a service fee, often known as a deductible.

Limitations and Exclusions: To understand what is and is not covered under a home warranty, carefully read the terms and conditions. Most warranties include limitations and exclusions, and certain pre-existing ailments may not be covered.

Peace of Mind: A home warranty can provide peace of mind by protecting you against unexpected repair costs for major home systems and appliances. It can be especially useful for first-time homebuyers who may lack the finances to handle major repair costs.

Finally, whether or not you need a house warranty is determined by your unique circumstances and level of risk tolerance. The warranty's cost should be weighed against the possible savings on repairs and peace of mind it provides.

WHAT'S THE DIFFERENCE BETWEEN A FIXED-RATE AND AN ADJUSTABLE-RATE MORTGAGE?

Mortgages are classified into two types: fixed-rate mortgages and adjustable-rate mortgages (ARMs). This is how they differ:

Fixed-Rate Mortgage: A fixed-rate mortgage has an interest rate that remains constant during the loan's term, which is commonly 15 or 30 years. This implies that your monthly mortgage payments will stay the same, giving stability and predictability throughout time. Fixed-rate mortgages are popular among homeowners who want the certainty that their mortgage payments will not alter.

Adjustable-Rate Mortgage (ARM): With an adjustable-rate mortgage, the interest rate is initially fixed for a set length of time, usually five, seven, or ten years, and then adjusted regularly based on market conditions. This means that your monthly mortgage payments may fluctuate over time, potentially increasing or decreasing due to changes in interest rates.

ARMs often have lower starting interest rates than fixed-rate mortgages, making them appealing to buyers who intend to sell or refinance before the original fixed period expires.

The decision between a fixed-rate mortgage and an adjustable-rate mortgage is influenced by your financial objectives, risk tolerance, and the length of time you intend to stay in the property. A fixed-rate mortgage provides stability and predictability, whereas an adjustable-rate mortgage (ARM) offers possible short-term savings but involves additional risk if interest rates rise later.

WHAT ARE CLOSING COSTS, AND WHO PAYS FOR THEM?

Closing costs are the fees and expenses connected with the completion of a real estate transaction. They typically range from 2% to 5% of the property's purchase price and cover a number of expenses, including:

Lender fees include loan origination, discount, and appraisal expenses.

Title fees cover title searches, title insurance, and closing agent services.

Government costs include recording fees, transfer taxes, and pre-paid property taxes.

Escrow Fees: These are fees for establishing an escrow account to keep funds for property taxes and homeowners' insurance.

Other fees may include home inspections, survey fees, and homeowner association dues.

Who pays for closing charges varies according to the terms of the purchase agreement and local norms? In rare situations, the buyer may agree to cover all or some of the closing fees as part of their offer. In other circumstances, the seller may agree to cover certain closing costs as a way to entice purchasers.

Buyers should budget for closing costs in addition to the down payment and other upfront expenses. Working with a qualified real estate agent and lender can help buyers understand their closing expenses and negotiate favorable conditions during the homebuying process.

WHAT IS PRIVATE MORTGAGE INSURANCE (PMI), AND DO I NEED IT?

Private Mortgage Insurance (PMI) is a type of insurance that lenders may demand borrowers to acquire if they are unable to put down at least 20% of the home's purchase price. Here's what you should know.

The purpose of PMI is to safeguard the lender in case the borrower defaults on the loan. It enables lenders to issue mortgages with lower down payment requirements, making homeownership more accessible to purchasers who do not have the money to cover a hefty down payment.

Cost: The cost of PMI varies depending on your down payment size, credit score, and mortgage type. PMI typically costs 0.3% to 1.5% of the original loan amount per year, and is included in your monthly mortgage payment.

Cancellation: The Homeowners Protection Act (HPA) requires lenders to automatically cancel PMI whenever your loan-to-value ratio (LTV) exceeds 78% of the original property value. You may also be able to request PMI cancellation after your LTV reaches 80%, which can be achieved by paying down your mortgage balance and increasing the value of your home.

Alternatives: If you can't make a 20% down payment, there are other financing choices that may allow you to avoid PMI. These may include piggyback loans, lender-paid mortgage insurance (LPMI), or government-backed loan programs like as FHA loans, which have their own mortgage insurance requirements.

Ultimately, whether or not you require PMI is determined by your unique financial circumstances and ambitions. While PMI can raise your monthly mortgage payment, it can also allow you to buy a property with a lower down payment, thus getting you into your home sooner.

HOW DO I CHOOSE THE RIGHT NEIGHBORHOOD FOR BUYING A HOME?

Choosing the correct neighborhood is an important consideration when purchasing a house because it may significantly affect your quality of life and property value. When analyzing neighborhoods, consider the following factors:

Consider the vicinity of job, schools, shopping, and public transportation. Consider your daily commute and whether the community provides convenient access to the amenities you require.

School District: Even if you don't have children, the quality of your local school district can influence property values. Research school ratings and performance to determine the quality of education in the area.

Safety is the most important factor to consider while choosing a neighborhood. Investigate crime rates, speak with local residents, and visit the area at various times of day to obtain a feel of the neighborhood's general safety and security.

Amenities and Lifestyle: Evaluate the neighborhood's amenities and recreational possibilities, including parks, restaurants, community centers, and cultural attractions. Consider whether the neighborhood matches your lifestyle and interests.

Property Values and Market Trends: Investigate the neighborhood's property values and market trends to determine how home values have increased over time. Look for indicators of expansion and development, which could suggest a healthy real estate market.

Future Development: Think about any upcoming or ongoing development initiatives in the neighborhood, such as new infrastructure, commercial developments, or zoning changes. These can have an impact on property values and the quality of life in the community.

Community Vibe: Pay attention to the area's sense of community and neighborliness. Are there any community activities, neighborhood associations, or local projects that promote a sense of belonging and connection among residents?

By carefully evaluating these variables and working with a competent real estate agent who understands the local market, you may discover the ideal neighborhood to fit your needs and improve your homeownership experience.

HOW CAN I KNOW WHETHER I'M READY TO BUY A HOUSE?

Ah, the age-old question: am I prepared to make the plunge into homeownership? It's a big choice, but here are several clues that you could be ready to buy a home:

Stable Finances: You have stable job and a consistent income that allows you to comfortably afford monthly mortgage payments, property taxes, homeowners insurance, and other homeownership obligations.

Savings for a Down Payment: You've saved enough for a down payment, ideally 20% of the home's purchase price, which will allow you to avoid private mortgage insurance (PMI) and qualify for better loan conditions.

You have a strong credit score, which qualifies you for a competitive interest rate on your mortgage. A higher credit score can help you save thousands of dollars in interest over the course of your loan.

Long-Term Plans: You intend to stay in the same area for the foreseeable future and are prepared to establish roots in a community. Buying a home is a long-term investment, so think about your future plans and ambitions.

Willingness to Take Responsibility: You are ready to accept the obligations of homeownership, such as maintenance and repairs, property taxes, and insurance. Owning a home involves time, effort, and financial commitment.

Market Conditions: You have done your research and understand the present situation of the real estate market. When you discover the ideal property in a competitive market, you are prepared to act fast and decisively.

Finally, the decision to buy a home is a personal one based on your own circumstances, aspirations, and desires. Take the time to carefully assess your preparation and consult with a reputable real estate expert who can offer advice and support throughout the home-buying process.

WHAT IS EARNEST MONEY, AND HOW DOES IT WORK?

Earnest money, also known as a good faith deposit, is a sum of money that a buyer pays to indicate their seriousness and commitment to purchase a property. This is how it works.

The purpose of earnest money is to demonstrate good confidence from the buyer to the seller. It implies that the buyer is serious about purchasing the property and gives the seller confidence that the buyer will complete the transaction.

The amount of earnest money required varies depending on the purchase price of the home, local customs, and discussions between the buyer and seller. Typically, earnest money ranges from 1% to 3% of the buying price.

Earnest money is normally deposited into an escrow account and held until the transaction is closed.

The escrow agent or closing attorney manages the earnest money deposit and guarantees that it is handled in accordance with the provisions of the purchase agreement.

Protection for the Seller: If the buyer cancels the transaction without a sufficient reason, the seller may be entitled to keep the earnest money as compensation for the time and effort wasted during the transaction. This protects the seller from customers who may not be sincere about finishing the transaction.

Earnest money may be refundable under certain conditions. For example, if the home inspection reveals severe faults that the seller refuses to remedy, the buyer may be able to cancel the transaction and demand a refund of their earnest money.

Applied Toward Closing Costs: At closing, the earnest money deposit is usually applied to the buyer's closing costs or down payment on the property. It reduces the amount of cash the buyer must bring to the closing table.

Overall, earnest money is a vital element of the home-buying process since it shows the buyer's commitment to the transaction and gives the seller confidence. Both parties must understand the terms of earnest money and how it will be handled if the contract is disputed or cancelled.

WHAT ARE HOME EQUITY LOANS AND LINES OF CREDIT (HELOCS)?

Home equity loans and home equity lines of credit (HELOCs) are two forms of loans that enable homeowners to borrow against the equity they have built up in their properties. Here's how they operate:

A home equity loan, sometimes known as a second mortgage, enables homeowners to borrow a lump sum of money using their house's equity as collateral. The loan is normally repaid over a set period of time with a fixed interest rate, comparable to a regular mortgage. Home equity loans are frequently utilized to cover substantial expenses such as home repairs, debt consolidation, and major purchases.

A Home Equity Line of Credit (HELOC) is a revolving line of credit that enables homeowners to borrow funds as needed, up to a predetermined credit limit, using their home equity as security.

Unlike a home equity loan, which gives a lump sum payment, a HELOC functions more like a credit card, allowing borrowers to borrow, repay, and borrow again as needed. HELOCs often have variable interest rates, which can change over time.

Both home equity loans and HELOCs can be beneficial financial instruments for homeowners who require cash for significant purchases or bills. However, it is critical to thoroughly weigh the risks and rewards of each loan type and borrow responsibly.

HOW CAN I IMPROVE MY CREDIT SCORE PRIOR TO BUYING A HOME?

Your credit score has a significant impact on your ability to qualify for a mortgage and obtain favorable loan conditions. Here are some suggestions to help you boost your credit score before purchasing a home:

Check your credit report. Begin by reviewing your credit reports from the three major credit agencies (Equifax, Experian, and TransUnion) for problems or inaccuracies. Dispute any errors you discover, and seek to fix any ongoing concerns that may be lowering your score.

Pay payments on Time: Your payment history has the greatest impact on your credit score, so make sure to pay all of your payments on time, every time. Create automatic payments or reminders to help you stay on track.

Reduce Debt: Pay down existing debt, particularly high-interest credit card debt, to lower your credit utilization ratio and enhance your credit score. Prioritize paying down balances with the highest interest rates first.

Avoid Opening New Accounts: Opening new credit accounts will temporarily lower your credit score, so avoid applying for new credit cards or loans in the months before applying for a mortgage.

Keep Old Accounts Open: Closing old credit accounts will decrease your credit history and lower your credit score, so keep them open even if you don't use them often.

Diversify Your Credit Mix: Having a variety of credit accounts, including credit cards, installment loans, and a mortgage, will boost your credit score. However, only take on new credit if it is financially viable for your situation.

Be Patient: Improving your credit score takes time, so be consistent in your efforts. Focus on developing good credit habits and managing your money properly.

Following these strategies and constantly monitoring your credit score will help you improve your creditworthiness and raise your chances of qualifying for a mortgage with favorable terms.

WHAT IS A HOME APPRAISAL, AND WHY IS IT IMPORTANT?

A house appraisal is an unbiased evaluation of a property's fair market value completed by a professional appraiser. Here's why it matters in the homebuying process:

Determining Market Value: The primary goal of a home appraisal is to assess the property's fair market value. Lenders demand an appraisal to confirm that the property's worth matches the amount of the loan requested by the buyer.

Protecting Lenders: An evaluation helps lenders avoid financing more than the property is worth. It decreases the lender's risk in the event that the borrower defaults on the loan and the property is auctioned to repay the outstanding debt.

An appraisal can also be used as a negotiating tactic between buyers and sellers. If the appraisal is lower than the agreed-upon purchase price, purchasers might use it to renegotiate the price or request repairs from the seller.

Mortgage Approval: In addition to determining the property's worth, lenders usually require an appraisal as part of the mortgage approval procedure.

Lenders evaluate the appraised value of the property to decide how much of a loan they are willing to lend the buyer.

Property Condition: While not the primary goal of an appraisal, appraisers may identify any substantial flaws or faults with the property that may affect its value. Buyers can utilize this information to make informed purchasing decisions.

Overall, a house assessment is a vital stage in the home-buying process that gives useful information to buyers, sellers, and lenders. It ensures that the purchase is based on an accurate valuation of the property and protects all parties involved.

WHAT ARE THE ADVANTAGES OF WORKING WITH A REAL ESTATE AGENT?

Working with a real estate agent can provide various benefits to both buyers and sellers. Here are some of the reasons you might want to consider working with a real estate agent:

Market Knowledge: Real estate brokers have extensive knowledge of the local market, including current trends, property valuations, and area amenities. They can offer significant insights and advice to help you make educated decisions.

Negotiation Skills: Real estate transactions need negotiation, and real estate agents are competent negotiators who can advocate on your behalf to ensure you obtain the best deal possible.

Real estate agents have access to a diverse selection of listings via the Multiple Listing Service (MLS) and other industry networks. They can assist you in finding properties that fit your criteria and scheduling viewings on your behalf.

Professional Network: Real estate agents have access to a network of experts such as bankers, inspectors, appraisers, and attorneys who can help with various stages of the transaction.

They can propose trustworthy professionals and arrange services to make the procedure more efficient.

Paperwork and Legal Guidance: Real estate transactions require a significant amount of paperwork, contracts, and legal documents. A real estate agent may help ensure that all paperwork is completed correctly and in accordance with applicable rules and regulations.

Peace of Mind: Buying or selling a house can be stressful, but having a real estate agent on your side can provide you peace of mind knowing that you are being guided through the process by an educated and experienced professional.

As a whole, engaging with a real estate agent can save you time, money, and bother while boosting the likelihood of a successful and easy transaction. A real estate agent can be a great resource and advocate throughout the home-buying or selling process.

WHAT ARE HOME EQUITY LOANS AND LINES OF CREDIT (HELOCS)?

Home equity loans and home equity lines of credit (HELOCs) are two forms of loans that enable homeowners to borrow against the equity they have built up in their properties. Here's how they operate:

A home equity loan, sometimes known as a second mortgage, enables homeowners to borrow a lump sum of money using their house's equity as collateral. The loan is normally repaid over a set period of time with a fixed interest rate, comparable to a regular mortgage. Home equity loans are frequently utilized to cover substantial expenses such as home repairs, debt consolidation, and major purchases.

A Home Equity Line of Credit (HELOC) is a revolving line of credit that enables homeowners to borrow funds as needed, up to a predetermined credit limit, using their home equity as security.

Unlike a home equity loan, which gives a lump sum payment, a HELOC functions more like a credit card, allowing borrowers to borrow, repay, and borrow again as needed. HELOCs often have variable interest rates, which can change over time.

Both home equity loans and HELOCs can be beneficial financial instruments for homeowners who require cash for significant purchases or bills. However, it is critical to thoroughly weigh the risks and rewards of each loan type and borrow responsibly.

HOW CAN I IMPROVE MY CREDIT SCORE PRIOR TO BUYING A HOME?

Your credit score has a significant impact on your ability to qualify for a mortgage and obtain favorable loan conditions. Here are some suggestions to help you boost your credit score before purchasing a home:

Check your credit report. Begin by reviewing your credit reports from the three major credit agencies (Equifax, Experian, and TransUnion) for problems or inaccuracies. Dispute any errors you discover, and seek to fix any ongoing concerns that may be lowering your score.

Pay payments on Time: Your payment history has the greatest impact on your credit score, so make sure to pay all of your payments on time, every time. Create automatic payments or reminders to help you stay on track.

Reduce Debt: Pay down existing debt, particularly high-interest credit card debt, to lower your credit utilization ratio and enhance your credit score. Prioritize paying down balances with the highest interest rates first.

Avoid Opening New Accounts: Opening new credit accounts will temporarily lower your credit score, so avoid applying for new credit cards or loans in the months before applying for a mortgage.

Keep Old Accounts Open: Closing old credit accounts will decrease your credit history and lower your credit score, so keep them open even if you don't use them often.

Diversify Your Credit Mix: Having a variety of credit accounts, including credit cards, installment loans, and a mortgage, will boost your credit score. However, only take on new credit if it is financially viable for your situation.

Be Patient: Improving your credit score takes time, so be consistent in your efforts. Focus on developing good credit habits and managing your money properly.

Following these strategies and constantly monitoring your credit score will help you improve your creditworthiness and raise your chances of qualifying for a mortgage with favorable terms.

WHAT IS A HOME APPRAISAL, AND WHY IS IT IMPORTANT?

A house appraisal is an unbiased evaluation of a property's fair market value completed by a professional appraiser. Here's why it matters in the homebuying process:

Determining Market Value: The primary goal of a home appraisal is to assess the property's fair market value. Lenders demand an appraisal to confirm that the property's worth matches the amount of the loan requested by the buyer.

Protecting Lenders: An evaluation helps lenders avoid financing more than the property is worth. It decreases the lender's risk in the event that the borrower defaults on the loan and the property is auctioned to repay the outstanding debt.

An appraisal can also be used as a negotiating tactic between buyers and sellers. If the appraisal is lower than the agreed-upon purchase price, purchasers might use it to renegotiate the price or request repairs from the seller.

Mortgage Approval: In addition to determining the property's worth, lenders usually require an appraisal as part of the mortgage approval procedure. Lenders evaluate the appraised value of the property to decide how much of a loan they are willing to lend the buyer.

Property Condition: While not the primary goal of an appraisal, appraisers may identify any substantial flaws or faults with the property that may affect its value. Buyers can utilize this information to make informed purchasing decisions.

Nevertheless, a house assessment is a vital stage in the home-buying process that gives useful information to buyers, sellers, and lenders. It ensures that the purchase is based on an accurate valuation of the property and protects all parties involved.

WHAT ARE THE ADVANTAGES OF WORKING WITH A REAL ESTATE AGENT?

Working with a real estate agent can provide various benefits to both buyers and sellers. Here are some of the reasons you might want to consider working with a real estate agent:

Market Knowledge: Real estate brokers have extensive knowledge of the local market, including current trends, property valuations, and area amenities. They can offer significant insights and advice to help you make educated decisions.

Negotiation Skills: Real estate transactions need negotiation, and real estate agents are competent negotiators who can advocate on your behalf to ensure you obtain the best deal possible.

Real estate agents have access to a diverse selection of listings via the Multiple Listing Service (MLS) and other industry networks. They can assist you in finding properties that fit your criteria and scheduling viewings on your behalf.

Professional Network: Real estate agents have access to a network of experts such as bankers, inspectors, appraisers, and attorneys who can help with various stages of the transaction.

They can propose trustworthy professionals and arrange services to make the procedure more efficient.

Paperwork and Legal Guidance: Real estate transactions require a significant amount of paperwork, contracts, and legal documents. A real estate agent may help ensure that all paperwork is completed correctly and in accordance with applicable rules and regulations.

Peace of Mind: Buying or selling a house can be stressful, but having a real estate agent on your side can provide you peace of mind knowing that you are being guided through the process by an educated and experienced professional.

Overall, engaging with a real estate agent can save you time, money, and bother while boosting the likelihood of a successful and easy transaction. A real estate agent can be a great resource and advocate throughout the home-buying or selling process

WHAT ARE SOME RED FLAGS TO LOOK OUT FOR WHEN BUYING A HOME?

When purchasing a home, it is critical to be aware of any potential red flags that may suggest underlying difficulties with the property. Here are some frequent red signs to look out for:

Structural Issues: Look for foundation cracks, sloping floors, or sagging walls. These issues can be costly to resolve and may suggest major structural flaws.

Water Damage: Water damage can cause mold and other health issues, so look for signs like water stains on walls or ceilings, musty aromas, or warped flooring. Check for leaks in plumbing fittings and around windows and doors.

Pest infestations, such as termites, rodents, or ants, can cause significant damage to a home if left untreated. Look for indicators of pest activity, such as droppings, chewed wood, or nests, and consider hiring a professional inspector to determine the severity of the infestation.

Poor upkeep: A poorly maintained home may be a red flag, indicating that the present owner has neglected or postponed upkeep. Look for evidence of neglect, such as overgrown vegetation, peeling paint, or out of date mechanical systems.

Neighborhood Issues: Pay attention to the neighborhood around the property and search for any red flags such as high crime rates, excessive noise or traffic, or dropping property prices. Visit the neighborhood at various times of day to get a sense of its overall vibe.

Title difficulties: Prior to closing on a home, it is critical to complete a title search to identify any potential title difficulties such as liens, encroachments, or easements. These flaws can muddle the title and impair your ownership rights, therefore they must be addressed before the transaction is finalized.

Environmental dangers: Be mindful of potential environmental dangers in the region, such as the presence of flood zones, landslides, or environmental contamination sites. These hazards can endanger people's health and safety, as well as reduce the value of the property.

By keeping an eye out for these red signs and performing extensive due diligence, you may avoid potential traps and make a more informed decision when purchasing a home.

HOW DOES THE HOME INSPECTION PROCESS WORK?

The home inspection procedure is an important phase in the homebuying process that allows purchasers to discover any hidden concerns with the property before closing. This is how it works.

Schedule the Inspection: Once you've signed a contract to buy a house, you usually have a window of time to schedule a home inspection. Hire a trained home inspector who has previously inspected properties identical to the one you're purchasing.

Attend the Inspection: Buyers can attend the house inspection, but it is not needed. Attending the inspection gives you the opportunity to ask questions, learn more about the property, and see any flaws firsthand.

Conduct the Inspection: The home inspector will completely inspect the property, including the exterior, interior, structural components, mechanical systems, and appliances. They will check for evidence of damage, faults, or safety issues and record their findings in a complete report.

Review the Inspection Report: Once the inspection is completed, the home inspector will present you with a written report summarizing their findings, including any faults detected during the examination. Review the report thoroughly and share any issues with your real estate agent.

Negotiate Repairs: If the inspection reveals any substantial flaws with the property, you may be able to negotiate repairs or credits with the seller. Your real estate agent can guide you through the process and advocate on your behalf.

determine on Next Steps: Based on the inspection results and any talks with the seller, you'll need to determine whether to proceed with the purchase, seek additional inspections, or walk away from the transaction.

As a whole, the home inspection process provides purchasers with vital information about the property's condition, allowing them to make more informed purchasing decisions. It's an important step in the home-buying process that can help preserve your investment and prevent costly surprises in the future.

HOW DO PROPERTY TAXES WORK FOR HOMEOWNERS?

Property taxes may not be the most glamorous issue, but they are an important aspect of homeownership. Let us break down how they work in simple terms:

Property taxes are taxes levied by local governments on the value of real properties. They are used to pay for public services such as schools, roads, and emergency services in your neighborhood.

Assessment: Your local government determines how much property taxes you owe by assessing the value of your property each year. This value is determined by the size of your property, its location, and recent sales of comparable homes in the neighborhood.

Tax Rate: After your property's value has been assessed, it is multiplied by the local tax rate to determine your property tax amount. Tax rates might vary greatly based on where you reside, so it's critical to understand the tax rate in your community.

Property taxes are usually paid annually or semiannually, depending on municipal restrictions. In other situations, they may be included in your monthly mortgage payment and held in an escrow account by your lender, who will then pay them for you.

Tax Exemptions and Deductions: Some homeowners may be qualified for tax breaks or deductions that will reduce their property taxes. These may include exemptions for older citizens, veterans, or disabled people, as well as deductions for home improvements or energy-efficient modifications.

Nonpayment Consequences: It is critical to pay your property taxes on time, as failure to do so can result in penalties, interest charges, and possibly the loss of your home due to tax foreclosure.

Overall, property taxes are a vital aspect of homeownership that contributes to the well-being of your neighborhood. Understanding how they function might help you budget effectively and avoid surprises at tax time.

WHAT IS A SELLER'S DISCLOSURE, AND WHY IS IT IMPORTANT?

A seller's disclosure is a document submitted by the seller that describes any known faults, issues, or concerns with the property for sale. Here's why it matters:

Full Disclosure: A seller's disclosure requires them to reveal any known faults or concerns with the property, such as structural issues, mechanical systems, appliances, or environmental risks. This enables purchasers to make more informed decisions about whether to proceed with the purchase.

Legal Requirement: In several states, sellers are obligated to disclose a seller's disclosure to prospective buyers. Failure to disclose known faults may subject the seller to legal liabilities and prospective lawsuits from buyers who discover unreported issues after the sale.

Due Diligence: A seller's disclosure is an important component of the due diligence process for purchasers.

It gives essential information about the property's condition and allows buyers to ask questions, conduct additional inspections, and negotiate repairs or credits with the seller as needed.

Buyer Protection: A seller's disclosure assists consumers avoid purchasing a property with concealed defects or issues that could be costly to address. Buyers can rest assured that the seller has been open and honest about the property's condition.

Documentation: A seller's disclosure documents the seller's assertions concerning the property's condition. If a dispute emerges after closing over unreported problems, the seller's disclosure can be used as evidence in court proceedings.

Overall, a seller's disclosure is a valuable document that promotes transparency and open communication between buyers and sellers. Buyers should thoroughly consider the seller's disclosure and ask questions about any difficulties or concerns before proceeding with the purchase.

WHAT IS ESCROW, AND HOW DOES IT WORK IN REAL ESTATE?

Escrow is a real estate transaction method that protects the interests of both purchasers and sellers by requiring all parties to fulfill their responsibilities before the deal is consummated. This is how it works.

After both the buyer and seller sign a purchase agreement, escrow is initiated with a neutral third party, usually an escrow or title business. To demonstrate good faith, the buyer's earnest money deposit is placed in escrow.

Deposit of cash and Documents: The buyer places the cash for the purchase, including the down payment and any additional closing charges, in escrow. The seller may also furnish the escrow holder with any essential documents, such as the property deed or house keys.

Title Search and Insurance: The escrow holder searches the property's title to guarantee that there are no liens, encumbrances, or ownership disputes. They also arrange for title insurance to safeguard the buyer and lender from any potential title difficulties.

Contingency time: During the contingency time specified in the purchase agreement, the buyer may conduct inspections, obtain financing, and verify the seller's disclosure. If any problems develop within this time, the buyer may seek repairs or credits from the vendor.

Closing Disclosure: Prior to closing, the escrow holder sends the buyer and seller a closing disclosure that details the final terms of the transaction, such as the purchase price, closing expenses, and any changes or prorations.

Closing: Once all contingencies are met, the buyer's lender finances the loan and prepares the closing documents. The buyer and seller sign the relevant documentation, and the escrow holder distributes the monies to the appropriate parties, including paying off any outstanding mortgages or liens on the property.

Recording: Following the closing, the escrow holder ensures that the deed and other legal paperwork are correctly recorded with the relevant government agency, transferring ownership of the property from seller to buyer.

Escrow facilitates real estate transactions in a secure and unbiased manner, ensuring that all parties fulfill their responsibilities and that the transaction runs quickly and efficiently.

WHAT IS A COUNTEROFFER IN REAL ESTATE?

A counteroffer in real estate is a seller's response to the buyer's original offer that details revisions to the terms of the purchase agreement. This is how it works.

Initial Offer: The buyer makes an initial offer on the property, specifying the purchase price, closing date, contingencies, and any other terms and circumstances.

Seller's Response: Rather of accepting or rejecting the buyer's offer directly, the seller may opt to counteroffer. The counteroffer often recommends adjustments to the previous offer's terms, such as a greater purchase price, a new closing date, or updated stipulations.

Negotiation: The buyer and seller continue to exchange counteroffers until they agree on all conditions of the purchase agreement.

This back-and-forth procedure may require numerous rounds of counteroffers until both sides are pleased with the terms.

Acceptance or Rejection: After both parties have agreed on the conditions of the purchase agreement, they sign the final contract, and the transaction proceeds to close. If either side is unable to agree on the terms, they may reject the counteroffer and walk away from the transaction.

Counteroffers are a regular component of the negotiation process in real estate transactions, allowing both buyers and sellers to work out the terms of the sale until they reach a mutually acceptable agreement.

WHAT IS A HOME WARRANTY AND SHOULD I BUY ONE?

A home warranty is a service contract that covers the repair or replacement of major household equipment and appliances. A house warranty, while not necessary, can provide homeowners with peace of mind and financial security. Here's what you should think about when selecting whether to buy a home warranty.

Coverage: Home warranties often include coverage for HVAC, plumbing, electrical, and major appliances such as refrigerators, dishwashers, and ovens. Some warranties may also include optional coverage for pool equipment and garage door openers.

Cost: The price of a home warranty varies depending on the level of coverage, the size of your property, and the provider. Typically, the annual premium ranges from a few hundred to a thousand dollars.

Service Calls: If a covered system or appliance fails, you will notify the warranty provider and file a claim. They will arrange for a service technician to come out and assess the problem. Each service call will normally incur a service fee, often known as a deductible.

Limitations and Exclusions: To understand what is and is not covered under a home warranty, carefully read the terms and conditions. Most warranties include limitations and exclusions, and certain pre-existing ailments may not be covered.

Peace of Mind: A home warranty can provide peace of mind by protecting you against unexpected repair costs for major home systems and appliances. It can be especially useful for first-time homebuyers who may lack the finances to handle major repair costs.

Finally, whether or not you should acquire a house warranty is determined by your specific circumstances and level of risk tolerance. The warranty's cost should be weighed against the possible savings on repairs and peace of mind it provides.

HOW DO PROPERTY TAXES WORK WHEN YOU BUY A HOME?

Property taxes are levied by local governments on real estate properties such as land and buildings. Here's how property taxes work when you buy a house:

Assessment is the process by which local taxing authorities calculate the taxable value of each property within their jurisdiction. This assessment is usually based on the property's size, location, and amenities.

Tax Rate: Once the taxable value of the property has been determined, the local government establishes a tax rate, also known as a millage rate or levy, that is used to compute the amount of property tax due. The tax rate is stated in mills, with one mill being one-tenth of one percent (0.001).

Payment plan: Property taxes are normally due annually, though the specific payment plan and due dates may differ depending on municipal restrictions. In some regions, property taxes can be paid in installments throughout the year.

Prorations: When purchasing a home, property taxes are frequently prorated between the buyer and seller based on the closing date.

The buyer pays the share of taxes owed for the time they will possess the property, whereas the seller pays the portion owed for the time they owned the property during the tax year.

Escrow Account: Many lenders require borrowers to escrow their property taxes and homeowners insurance with their monthly mortgage payment. The lender collects cash from the borrower on a monthly basis and pays property taxes and insurance on their behalf when due.

Appeals Process: If you believe your property has been over-assessed or disagree with the amount of property taxes owing, you may be able to appeal the assessment using a formal process described by your local taxation authority.

Property taxes pay local government services and infrastructure, such as schools, public safety, and road upkeep. Homeowners should understand how property taxes are calculated and paid in order to comply with municipal requirements.

WHAT IS A CLOSING DISCLOSURE, AND WHY IS IT IMPORTANT?

A closing disclosure is a five-page document that details the final terms and costs of a mortgage loan, such as the loan amount, interest rate, closing costs, and other fees. Here's why it matters in the homebuying process:

Transparency: The closing disclosure clarifies the terms and costs of the mortgage loan. It enables borrowers to check and compare the final terms with the loan estimate provided by the lender at the start of the procedure.

Compliance: The Consumer Financial Protection Bureau (CFPB) requires closing disclosures under the Truth in Lending Act (TILA) and the Real Estate Settlement Procedures Act (RESPA). Lenders must present borrowers with a closing disclosure at least three working days before closing to allow them time to evaluate the conditions and raise questions.

Accuracy: The closing disclosure should accurately represent the loan's final terms, such as the loan amount, interest rate, monthly payment, and closing charges.

Any differences between the closing disclosure and the loan estimate must be rectified prior to closing.

Borrowers can protect themselves by examining the closing disclosure and ensuring that no unexpected fees or expenditures are levied at closing. It enables borrowers to discover and resolve any problems or conflicts with the lender before closing the transaction.

Borrowers can utilize the closing disclosure to compare the loan's final terms and fees to the loan estimate supplied by their lender. If there are major variations between the two documents, borrowers may be able to renegotiate or walk away from their loan.

Education: The closing disclosure allows borrowers to ask questions and get explanation on any terms or fees that they don't understand. Borrowers should completely comprehend the conditions of their mortgage loan before closing to avoid any surprises later.

Overall, the closing disclosure is an essential document in the home-buying process that informs borrowers about the terms and costs of their mortgage loan. Borrowers should thoroughly consider the closing disclosure and ask questions about anything they don't understand before closing on the loan.

HOW DO I DETERMINE MY DEBT-TO-INCOME RATIO (DTI) FOR MORTGAGES?

Your debt-to-income ratio (DTI) is an important element for lenders when determining your eligibility for a home loan. It compares your monthly debt payments to your total monthly income. Here is how to determine your DTI.

Add Up Your Monthly Debt Payments: Begin by adding up all of your monthly debt payments, such as:

- ❖ Mortgage or rent payments.
- ❖ Automobile loans
- ❖ Student loans
- ❖ Minimum credit card payments.
- ❖ Personal loans
- ❖ Child support and alimony payments

Calculate your gross monthly income. Next, determine your gross monthly income, which is your entire earnings before taxes and any deductions. This may include earnings from sources such as:

- ❖ Salary or wages?
- ❖ Bonuses or commission
- ❖ Rental and investment income
- ❖ Social security or disability benefits.

Divide your monthly debt payments by your monthly gross income. Finally, divide your total monthly debt payments by your gross monthly income, then multiply the result by 100 to get a percentage. The formula looks like this:

> DTI = (Total Monthly Debt Payments/Gross Monthly Income) x 100.

DTI is calculated by multiplying gross monthly income by total monthly debt payments.

For example, if your total monthly debt payments are $1,500 and your gross monthly income is $5,000, your DTI will be:

> $DTI = (1,500 / 5,000) \times 100 = 30\%$
>
> DTI= (5,000 1,500)×100=30%

Interpret Your DTI: Lenders prefer borrowers with a DTI of 43% or below, while some loan programs may accept higher DTIs. A lower DTI shows that you have more income available to meet your loan obligations, making you a less risky borrower in the eyes of lenders.

Calculating your DTI before applying for a mortgage will give you a better picture of your financial situation and how much you can afford to borrow. If your DTI is high, you may need to reduce your debt or increase your income in order to qualify for a mortgage with favorable conditions.

WHAT ARE SOME TYPICAL CLOSING COSTS FOR BUYING A HOME?

Closing costs are fees and expenses incurred when acquiring a home at the closing table. Closing fees might vary depending on the home's purchase price and location. However, you should be aware of the following frequent closing costs:

Loan Origination Fee: This fee covers the administrative costs associated with processing and underwriting your mortgage loan.

Appraisal Fee: Lenders typically seek an appraisal to determine the property's value, and borrowers are responsible for paying for it.

Title insurance is typically purchased by both lenders and buyers to protect themselves against potential title issues such as liens, encumbrances, or ownership disputes.

Home Inspection Fee: Although it is not necessarily required, many purchasers prefer to have a professional home inspection performed to assess the property's condition and identify any potential issues.

Legal Expenses: In some areas, buyers may need to hire an attorney to oversee the closing process and ensure the accuracy of all legal documents.

Recording Fees: These fees cover the cost of registering the deed and other legal documents with the appropriate government body to transfer title of the property.

Escrow or title companies, like financial advisors, typically charge fees for their services in overseeing the closing process and managing funds in escrow.

Buyers are often required to make upfront payments for a variety of expenditures throughout the closing process. Property taxes, homeowners insurance, and mortgage loan prepaid interest are some examples of these fees.

Homeowners Association (HOA) Fees: If the property is part of a homeowners association, buyers may be required to pay any outstanding HOA dues or fees at closing.

Transfer Taxes: Some states and municipalities levy transfer or conveyance taxes on real estate transactions, which are usually shared between the buyer and seller.

Buyers should budget for closing costs in addition to their down payment and other home-buying expenses. Your lender or real estate agent can offer you with a thorough estimate of closing expenses depending on your unique circumstances.

WHAT IS PRIVATE MORTGAGE INSURANCE (PMI), AND DO I NEED IT?

Private Mortgage Insurance (PMI) is a type of insurance that lenders demand borrowers to acquire if they put down less than 20% on a standard mortgage loan. PMI protects the lender in the event that the borrower defaults on the loan and the property goes into foreclosure. Here's everything you need know about PMI:

Cost: The cost of PMI varies depending on your down payment size, credit score, and mortgage loan type. PMI typically costs between 0.3% and 1.5% of the original loan amount per year, payable in monthly installments.

Cancellation: Once you have enough equity in your home—typically when your loan-to-value (LTV) ratio hits 80%—you may be able to cancel your PMI. Alternatively, if you are current on your mortgage payments, PMI will automatically stop when your LTV ratio reaches 78% of the original property value.

Down Payment: Making a higher down payment may allow you to avoid or minimize the cost of PMI. For example, if you make a 10% or 15% down payment rather than the required 3% to 5%, your PMI premiums may be reduced.

Loan Types: PMI is normally required for traditional mortgages with down payments of less than 20%. Government-backed loans, such as FHA and USDA loans, have separate mortgage insurance requirements that may differ from PMI.

PMI premiums may be tax deductible for qualified borrowers, subject to income limits and other conditions. Consult a tax professional to see if you are eligible for this deduction.

While PMI raises the cost of homeownership, it can make it more affordable for purchasers who cannot make a significant down payment up front. When deciding on a mortgage and budgeting for homeownership, keep the cost of PMI in mind.

WHAT IS A HOME EQUITY LINE OF CREDIT (HELOC), AND HOW DOES IT WORK?

A property Equity Line of Credit (HELOC) is a sort of revolving credit that enables homeowners to borrow against the equity they have accumulated in their property. This is how it works.

Access to Funds: A HELOC allows homeowners to borrow funds as needed, up to a predetermined credit limit, and use their home equity as security. Borrowers can access funds by writing checks, using a debit card, or sending money online.

Repayment: During the draw period, which normally lasts 5 to 10 years, borrowers can make interest-only payments on the loan. After the draw time has ended, the HELOC enters the repayment phase, during which borrowers must repay both the principle and interest on the outstanding sum.

Variable Interest Rate: HELOCs usually feature variable interest rates that are linked to a benchmark rate, like the prime rate. This means that the interest rate and monthly payment amount may change over time, thereby raising the cost of borrowing.

Flexible Fund Use: Borrowers can use HELOC money for a variety of objectives, including home upgrades, debt consolidation, education fees, and unforeseen needs.

Tax Deductibility: In certain circumstances, the interest paid on a HELOC may be tax deductible, subject to certain limitations and restrictions. Consult a tax professional to see if you are eligible for this deduction.

Foreclosure danger: Failure to repay a HELOC, like any other house-secured loan, can end in foreclosure, putting your home at danger. Borrow sensibly, and only take out a HELOC if you can afford to repay it.

HELOCs can be an effective financial tool for homeowners who require cash for major costs or investments. However, it is critical to thoroughly weigh the risks and rewards of a HELOC and borrow wisely based on your unique financial position.

WHAT'S THE DISTINCTION BETWEEN A FIXED-RATE MORTGAGE AND AN ADJUSTABLE-RATE MORTGAGE (ARM)?

Fixed-rate mortgages (FRMs) and adjustable-rate mortgages (ARMs) are two popular types of mortgage loans, both with perks and downsides. This is how they differ:

Fixed-rate mortgages:

Fixed-rate mortgages have an interest rate that remains constant during the loan's term, which is often 15 or 30 years. This implies that your monthly principal and interest payment will be the same each month, giving stability and certainty.

Monthly Payments: Because the interest rate is fixed, so are your monthly mortgage payments, making it easier to budget and plan for homeownership expenses.

Long-Term Stability: Fixed-rate mortgages are perfect for borrowers who value long-term stability and predictability in their mortgage payments, particularly during periods of rising interest rates.

Fixed-rate mortgages often have higher initial interest rates than ARMs, making them more expensive in the short run.

Adjustable Rate Mortgage (ARM):

Interest Rate: An adjustable rate mortgage (ARM) has a variable interest rate that can fluctuate over time based on changes in a set benchmark rate, such as the prime rate or the London Interbank Offered Rate.

Initial Rate term: Most ARMs have an initial fixed-rate term during which the interest rate remains steady for a specific amount of time, usually 5, 7, or 10 years. Following the first time, the interest rate is adjusted monthly based on market conditions.

Lower starting Interest Rates: ARMs often offer lower starting interest rates than fixed-rate mortgages, making them more affordable in the short term. However, debtors should be prepared for larger payments once the initial time expires.

Payment Changes: Because interest rates can fluctuate over time, your monthly mortgage payment may rise or fall in response to interest rate movements. This can make budgeting more difficult, especially if rates climb dramatically.

When deciding between a fixed-rate mortgage and an ARM, you should examine your financial goals, risk tolerance, and future plans. If you seek consistency and predictability, a fixed-rate mortgage could be the best option. If you're okay with some volatility and want to take advantage of lower beginning rates, an ARM can be worth considering.

WHAT'S THE DIFFERENCE BETWEEN A CONVENTIONAL LOAN AND A GOVERNMENT-BACKED LOAN?

Conventional loans and government-backed loans are the two main forms of mortgage loans, each with its own eligibility rules, loan limits, and terms. This is how they differ:

Conventional Loan:

Lender: The government does not insure or guarantee conventional loans. Instead, they are originated and funded by private lenders such as banks, credit unions, and mortgage firms.

Down Payment: Conventional loans normally require a down payment of at least 3% to 20% of the purchase price, while applicants with excellent credit may be eligible for a smaller down payment.

Private mortgage insurance (PMI): Borrowers with a down payment of less than 20% on a traditional loan are typically required to obtain private mortgage insurance (PMI) to protect the lender in the event of default.

Credit Score: Conventional loans often have tighter credit score requirements than government-backed loans, with minimum credit scores ranging from 620 to 680, depending on the lender and loan type.

Government-backed loans:

The Federal Housing Administration (FHA), the Department of Veterans Affairs (VA), or the United States Department of Agriculture (USDA) insures or guarantees government-backed loans.

Down Payment: Government-backed loans frequently need lower down payments than conventional loans. For example, FHA loans require a 3.5% down payment, whereas VA and USDA loans may give 0% down payment choices to qualified customers.

Mortgage Insurance: Government-backed loans may require mortgage insurance charges, comparable to PMI on conventional loans, to safeguard the lender against default. However, the requirements and cost of mortgage insurance may differ depending on the loan type and the borrower's creditworthiness.

Credit Score: Government-backed loans typically have more flexible credit score requirements than traditional loans, making them available to borrowers with lower credit scores or less established credit histories.

When deciding between a conventional loan and a government-backed loan, borrowers should examine their credit score, down payment amount, and eligibility for certain lending programs. To obtain the ideal mortgage solution for your specific demands and financial circumstances, you should shop around and compare loan possibilities from several lenders.

WHAT IS EARNEST MONEY, AND WHY IS IT IMPORTANT IN REAL ESTATE TRANSACTIONS?

Earnest money is a deposit provided by a buyer to show their sincere intent to acquire a property. It is often paid upfront when the purchase agreement is signed and held in escrow until the transaction is completed. Here's why earnest money matters in a real estate transaction:

Demonstrates Buyer Commitment: By contributing earnest money, the buyer demonstrates to the seller that they are serious about purchasing the property and have the financial resources to do so. It helps to show the buyer's dedication to the transaction.

Earnest money protects the seller in the event that the buyer cancels the transaction without a justifiable reason. If the buyer fails to carry out their obligations under the purchase agreement, such as completing inspections or obtaining financing, the seller may be entitled to retain the earnest money as recompense for their time and inconvenience.

Negotiating Tool: The buyer's earnest money offer can be used to negotiate during the offer process.

A higher earnest money deposit may indicate to the seller that the buyer is financially secure and committed to the transaction, making their offer more appealing.

Earnest money is often used to cover the buyer's down payment or closing charges when the transaction is completed. It decreases the amount of cash required by the buyer at the closing table and can help defray transaction charges.

Risk for Buyer: While earnest money protects the seller, it also exposes the buyer to financial risk. If the buyer fails to meet their duties under the purchase agreement without a justifiable reason, they may forfeit their earnest money to the seller.

Ultimately, earnest money is an important part of a real estate deal because it shows the buyer's commitment to the purchase and provides some protection for the seller. Both parties must comprehend the terms and circumstances of earnest money as stipulated in the purchase agreement.

WHAT IS A COMPARATIVE MARKET ANALYSIS (CMA), AND WHY IS IT USEFUL?

A Comparative Market Analysis (CMA) is a strategy used by real estate brokers to assess a property's fair market value by comparing it to recently sold properties in the same area. Why is a CMA useful?

Determines Market Value: A CMA assists sellers in determining the best listing price for their home based on current market conditions and recent sales of similar properties. The realtor can determine the fair market value of the property by examining data from similar residences in the region.

Sets realistic expectations: While sellers may have a certain price in mind for their property, a CMA gives an objective review of market worth based on recent sales data. It helps sellers set reasonable expectations and avoids overpricing, which can repel potential buyers.

A CMA helps sellers design a price strategy that considers market trends, competition, and the condition of the property. It enables sellers to position their property competitively in the market, attracting possible purchasers.

A CMA assists purchasers in making offers by providing vital information about the fair market value of properties they are interested in purchasing. It allows them to make more educated selections when submitting offers and negotiating with sellers.

A CMA evaluates market trends by assessing recent sales data and patterns in the local real estate market, revealing information about inventory levels, days on market, and buyer desire. This information can help buyers and sellers understand market dynamics.

As a whole, a Comparative Market Analysis (CMA) is an invaluable resource for both buyers and sellers in the real estate industry. It offers an impartial assessment of a property's market value based on recent sales data, assisting sellers in setting realistic pricing expectations and guiding purchasers in making educated judgments.

WHAT IS A HOMEOWNERS ASSOCIATION (HOA), AND WHAT ARE ITS RESPONSIBILITIES?

A Homeowners Association (HOA) is a group formed by a real estate developer or local people to manage and control a residential community, such as a condominium complex, planned community, or gated neighborhood. Here's all you should know about HOAs and their responsibilities:

Community Management: An HOA's major role is to manage and maintain the community's common areas and amenities, including parks, playgrounds, swimming pools, and clubhouses. The HOA is responsible for ensuring that these places are well-maintained and accessible to residents.

Enforcement of Rules and Regulations: HOAs often have a set of rules and regulations called covenants, conditions, and restrictions (CC&Rs) that control how properties in the community can be used and maintained. The HOA is in charge of enforcing these laws and resolving violators with fines, warnings, or other means.

HOAs collect regular dues and assessments from homeowners to pay the community's maintenance and operation. These money are used to pay for expenses such as landscaping, repairs, insurance, utilities, and administration.

Budgeting and financial management: The HOA is responsible for developing an annual budget outlining estimated spending and revenue streams for the following fiscal year.

They are also in charge of handling the association's finances, which include collecting dues, paying bills, and keeping reserves for future needs.

Community Events and Activities: Some homeowners associations conduct community events and activities to help people feel more connected to one another. These could include Christmas parties, social gatherings, recreational events, and instructional programs.

Architectural Review: Many homeowners associations include an architectural review committee that analyzes and approves planned changes to the exterior of homes in the neighborhood, such as additions, renovations, or landscaping enhancements. This contributes to the aesthetic integrity of the community and protects property values.

Dispute Resolution: The HOA may also act as a mediator in issues between homeowners, such as noise complaints, parking conflicts, or disagreements over common amenities. They may have a procedure in place to settle conflicts and address issues among inhabitants.

Nevertheless, a Homeowners Association (HOA) is critical in sustaining and managing residential communities by ensuring that common areas are well-maintained, laws are followed, and property values are preserved. Before purchasing a property within a HOA, homebuyers should thoroughly research the association's rules, fees, and duties.

WHAT IS TITLE INSURANCE, AND WHY IS IT IMPORTANT?

Title insurance is a type of insurance that protects homeowners and lenders from financial losses caused by flaws in the title of a property. Here's why title insurance is essential in a real estate deal.

Title insurance protects against a variety of title problems that may impact the homeowner's ownership rights or the lender's security interest in the property. These flaws could include errors or omissions in the public record, undisclosed liens or encumbrances, forgeries or fraud in the chain of title, or competing ownership claims.

Ownership Rights: Title insurance guarantees that the homeowner has clear and marketable title to the property, free of any legal or financial encumbrances that could jeopardize their ownership rights or capacity to sell or refinance it in the future.

Lender Protection: Lenders often ask borrowers to obtain lender's title insurance to safeguard their security interest in the property.

Lender's title insurance protects the outstanding balance of the mortgage loan in the event that the lender's security interest is challenged owing to a title flaw.

Title insurance gives homeowners and lenders peace of mind since it protects them from unforeseen title concerns that may develop after the closing. It offers them confidence that their investment in the property is safe and that they will not suffer financial losses as a result of title flaws.

Cost-Effective Protection: The one-time charge for title insurance is minimal when compared to the possible financial losses caused by a title flaw. Purchasing title insurance is an affordable approach to reduce the risks connected with title issues and ensure a smooth and secure real estate transaction.

Coverage Beyond Closing: Unlike other types of insurance, title insurance covers past occurrences that may have an impact on the title's validity. It is in force for as long as the homeowner or lender has an interest in the property.

Nevertheless, title insurance is a necessary component of any real estate transaction since it protects homeowners and lenders from the risks connected with title problems. It offers peace of mind and financial security by assuring that the property's title is clear and marketable.

WHAT IS A HOME INSPECTION, AND WHY IS IT IMPORTANT?

A house inspection is a detailed evaluation of a property's condition, usually performed by a qualified home inspector, to uncover any problems or deficiencies that could jeopardize its safety, integrity, or worth. Here's why a home inspection is necessary in the homebuying process:

Identifies Hidden flaws: A home inspection reveals any hidden flaws or defects in the property that might not be obvious to the naked eye. This covers issues with the construction, foundation, roof, plumbing, electrical systems, HVAC systems, appliances, and so on.

Ensures Safety and Security: A home inspection helps to verify that the house is safe and secure for the buyer and their family. It detects potential risks or safety concerns, such as electrical hazards, mold, asbestos, radon gas, or structural flaws that must be corrected.

A home inspection educates the buyer by providing useful information and insights into the property's condition. It helps purchasers understand the home's components and systems, how they work, and what maintenance or repairs may be required in the future.

negotiation Tool: The results of the house inspection can be utilized as a negotiation tool during the home-buying process. If substantial defects are discovered, the buyer may request repairs, credits, or a price reduction from the seller to resolve them.

Budgeting for Repairs: A home inspection report includes a thorough list of necessary repairs and maintenance jobs. This enables the buyer to budget for future repairs and prioritize required changes after closing.

Peace of Mind: A home inspection gives the buyer peace of mind that they are making an informed selection on the property. It reassures them that the house is in good condition and that there are no big problems that could cause a financial burden or a safety risk.

In general, a home inspection is an important stage in the house-buying process since it allows purchasers to make informed decisions while also protecting their investment in the property. It provides crucial information about the home's condition and lets purchasers to rectify any faults before making the final purchase.

WHAT COMMON RED FLAGS SHOULD YOU LOOK FOR DURING A HOME INSPECTION?

During a home inspection, keep an eye out for potential red flags that could suggest serious problems with the property. Here are some frequent red signs to watch for:

Water Damage: Stains on walls or ceilings, musty aromas, warped floors, or apparent mold growth may indicate leaks, plumbing problems, or inadequate drainage on the property.

Structural Issues: Cracks in the foundation, walls, or ceilings, uneven flooring, or doors and windows that stick or do not shut properly may signal structural issues that are costly to repair.

Roof Problems: Missing or broken roof shingles, sagging or uneven roof lines, signs of water penetration in the attic, or evidence of roof leaks can all signal roof issues that need to be repaired or replaced.

Electrical Issues: Outdated or hazardous electrical systems, such as overloaded circuits, exposed wire, or defective outlets and switches, can cause fires and should be repaired by a competent electrician.

Plumbing Concerns: Low water pressure, slow drains, leaky faucets or pipes, or evidence of water stains or corrosion around plumbing fixtures may signal a problem that has to be repaired.

HVAC System Defects: Inadequate heating or cooling, strange noises or aromas from the HVAC system, or obvious traces of rust or corrosion on heating or cooling equipment may indicate HVAC system issues that need to be addressed.

Pest Infestations: Pest evidence, such as droppings, gnaw marks, or obvious termite damage, might indicate a pest infestation, necessitating professional removal and repair.

Visible mold or mildew development, musty aromas, or indicators of water damage may indicate moisture problems that can lead to mold growth, posing health risks and necessitating cleanup.

Foundation Problems: Cracks in the foundation, uneven settling, or symptoms of moisture penetration in the basement or crawl space can all signal foundation issues that could jeopardize the home's stability.

Improper Drainage: Poor drainage surrounding the property, standing water in the yard or basement, or erosion indicators may indicate drainage problems that could result in water damage or floods.

It's crucial to note that not all faults discovered during a home inspection are deal-breakers, but they may necessitate further investigation or negotiation with the seller. A trained home inspector can help detect potential red flags and make recommendations for how to handle them.

WHAT IS AN ESCALATION CLAUSE IN A REAL ESTATE OFFER?

An escalation clause is a condition in a real estate offer that permits the buyer to automatically boost their offer price above rival offers up to a certain limit. Here's how an escalation clause operates:

Base Offer: The buyer makes a base offer to acquire the property at a certain price, usually slightly higher than the asking price.

Escalation Provision: The escalation clause includes a provision saying that the buyer's offer will automatically grow by a predetermined increment above any competing offers, up to a buyer-set maximum price.

Competing Offers: If another buyer makes a competing bid on the property, the escalation clause is triggered, and the buyer's price is immediately increased by the set amount over the competing offer.

Maximum Price: The escalation clause specifies the maximum price the buyer is ready to pay for the property. If the rival offer surpasses the buyer's maximum price, the escalation clause is no longer applicable, and the buyer's offer remains at the base price.

Verification of rival Offer: In most cases, the seller must produce verification of the rival offer in order to trigger the escalation clause. This could include a copy of the rival offer or a signed declaration from the seller's agent that confirms the conditions of the offer.

Seller Acceptance: The seller might accept the buyer's increased offer or counteroffer with different terms. When reviewing offers, the seller may take into account the buyer's finance strength, closing timeline, and other stipulations.

Escalation clauses can be a beneficial weapon for purchasers competing in a hot real estate market with many offers on prime homes. However, buyers must carefully assess the dangers and benefits of incorporating an escalation clause in their offer, as well as seek advice from their real estate agent or attorney.

WHAT IS DUAL AGENCY IN REAL ESTATE? IS IT LEGAL?

Dual agency happens when a real estate agent or firm represents both the buyer and seller in a single real estate transaction. In a dual agency arrangement, the agent has fiduciary duties to both parties, such as loyalty, secrecy, and full disclosure of material facts. Here's all you should know about dual agency:

Representation of Both Parties: In a dual agency arrangement, the agent or brokerage acts as both the buyer and seller in the transaction. This means the agent has a duty of loyalty and fiduciary responsibility to both parties.

Conflict of Interest: Dual agency raises worries about potential conflicts of interest because the agent's loyalty is split between the buyer and the seller. For example, the agent may have access to secret information from one party that could either benefit or hinder the other side.

Disclosure Requirements: In many countries, real estate agents must disclose their agency affiliation to both parties and receive written consent from both parties before proceeding with dual agency representation.

This enables buyers and sellers to make more informed decisions about whether to agree to dual agency.

Limited Representation: In some situations, dual agency may result in limited representation, in which the agent serves as a facilitator rather than an advocate for either party. In this case, the agent may provide administrative assistance and encourage communication between the parties but does not offer advocacy or advice.

Legal Considerations: While dual agency is permitted in many places, it is subject to rules and limits designed to safeguard the interests of both buyers and sellers. Some states outright prohibit dual agency, while others allow it with specified conditions and disclosure requirements.

Alternative Options: When dual agency is not authorized or advisable, buyers and sellers can deal with different agents from the same brokerage or hire their own independent representation.

Dual agency can be a complicated and contentious practice in real estate, raising questions about conflicts of interest and impartiality. Buyers and sellers must grasp the consequences of dual agency and carefully weigh their options when selecting representation in a real estate transaction.

WHAT IS A HOME WARRANTY, AND IS IT WORTH BUYING?

A house warranty is a service agreement that covers the repair or replacement of major home systems and appliances due to normal wear and tear. Here's everything you need to know about home warranties and if they're worth buying:

Home warranties often include coverage for HVAC (heating, ventilation, and air conditioning), plumbing, electrical, and major appliances such as refrigerators, ovens, dishwashers, and washing machines. Some home warranty policies may provide optional coverage for additional things such as pool equipment or garage door openers.

Cost: The cost of a house warranty varies according to the degree of coverage, the size and location of the home, and the provider. Home warranty plans normally cost between a few hundred to a thousand dollars per year, with a service call fee for each repair or replacement claim.

Claims Process: When a covered item fails or malfunctions, the homeowner contacts the home warranty company. The company deploys a licensed contractor or service expert to diagnose the problem and determine whether it is covered by the warranty.

If the repair or replacement is covered, the homeowner is responsible for the service call fee, while the warranty company covers the repair or replacement costs.

Benefits: Home warranties can give homeowners peace of mind by covering unexpected repair costs for major home systems and appliances. They can also be beneficial to purchasers purchasing a resale house because they cover older systems and appliances that may be nearing the end of their lives.

Limitations and Exclusions: Carefully read the terms and conditions of a home warranty policy, as they may contain limitations, exclusions, and coverage caps. Pre-existing conditions, cosmetic flaws, and incorrect maintenance may not be covered by the guarantee.

Value Proposition: Whether or not a house warranty is worthwhile depends on the age and condition of the home, the cost of the guarantee, and the homeowner's risk tolerance. Some homeowners may enjoy the piece of mind and financial security given by a house warranty, whilst others may want to self-insure and save money for prospective repairs.

Ultimately, the decision to acquire a home warranty is based on your unique circumstances, tastes, and budget. It is critical to thoroughly assess the cost and coverage of a home warranty plan and determine whether it meets your needs and objectives as a homeowner.

WHAT ARE SOME COMMON CLOSING COSTS IN REAL ESTATE TRANSACTIONS?

Closing costs are fees and expenses incurred during the acquisition or sale of a property that are normally paid at the transaction's closing or settlement. Here are some typical closing costs in a real estate transaction:

The Loan Origination Fee covers the administrative costs of processing and underwriting the mortgage loan. It is usually represented as a percentage of the loan amount.

Appraisal Fee: Lenders require an appraisal to assess the property's fair market value. The buyer normally pays for the appraisal, which is carried out by a licensed appraiser.

Title insurance protects both the buyer and the lender from financial losses caused by problems in the property's title.

Title insurance is classified into two types: lender's title insurance, which protects the lender's interest in the property, and owner's title insurance, which safeguards the buyer's ownership rights.

Attorney Fees: In some states, buyers and sellers can retain attorneys to represent their interests during the transaction. Attorney fees vary based on the complexity of the transaction and the attorney's hourly rate.

Home Inspection Fee: Typically, the buyer pays for a professional home inspection to analyze the property's condition and identify any faults or defects that may need to be repaired.

Recording costs: The local government charges costs for recording the deed and other legal documents linked to the transfer of ownership of the property.

Escrow Fees: Escrow fees pay the cost of the escrow service, which allows the buyer, seller, and lender to transfer monies and documents seamlessly. Prior to closing, the escrow company guarantees that all parties have fulfilled their commitments under the purchase agreement.

Property Taxes: Depending on when the closing occurs, the buyer may be required to pay a prorated amount of the current year's property taxes.

Prepaid Interest: The buyer may be required to pay prepaid interest at closing to cover the mortgage loan's interest from the closing date until the end of each month.

Homeowners Association (HOA) Fees: If the property is in a community with a homeowners association, the buyer may be required to pay prorated HOA dues at closing.

Survey Fee: The buyer may be required to pay for a survey of the property to validate the boundary lines and identify any encroachments or easements.

Courier Fees: These are the fees charged for courier services that transport papers between the parties engaged in the transaction.

Closing fees vary depending on the property's location, purchase amount, and kind of mortgage loan. Buyers and sellers should carefully consider the projected closing fees provided by their lender or closing agent and budget accordingly.

WHAT IS A HOME EQUITY LINE OF CREDIT (HELOC), AND HOW DOES IT WORK?

A Home Equity Line of Credit (HELOC) is a revolving loan that allows homeowners to borrow against the equity in their home. This is how a HELOC works:

Equity is the difference between the home's current market value and the amount owed on the mortgage. For example, if the house is worth $300,000 and the mortgage balance is $200,000, the homeowner has $100,000 in equity.

Credit Limit: When a homeowner applies for a HELOC, the lender determines the credit limit based on the amount of equity in the property, as well as other variables such as the borrower's credit history and income. The homeowner may borrow from the line of credit as needed, up to the credit limit.

Draw Period: The draw period is the initial term during which the homeowner can access funds from the HELOC, which normally lasts 5 to 10 years. During the draw period, the homeowner may borrow funds and make interest-only payments on the borrowed amount.

Repayment time: After the draw time ends, the HELOC enters the repayment period, during which the homeowner is no longer able to borrow cash and must repay the outstanding sum. The repayment period typically ranges from 10 to 20 years and may include both principal and interest installments.

HELOCs often have a variable interest rate, which implies that the rate might alter over time due to market fluctuations. The interest rate is often based on a benchmark rate, such as the prime rate, plus a margin specified by the lender.

Homeowners can access funds from their HELOC in a variety of ways, including writing checks, using a debit card linked to the account, or transferring funds electronically. Borrowers can use the cash for a variety of reasons, including home improvements, debt consolidation, educational expenses, and unanticipated crises.

A HELOC, like a mortgage loan, uses the borrower's home as security. If the borrower fails to repay the loan in accordance with the terms of the agreement, the lender may foreclose on the property to recover the remaining debt.

Tax Deductibility: In some situations, interest paid on a HELOC may be tax deductible if the funds are used for home improvements that increase the property's value. However, tax laws governing HELOC interest deductions have changed in recent years, so homeowners should consult with a tax adviser for advice.

Overall, a Home Equity Line of Credit (HELOC) is a flexible and handy way for homeowners to obtain funds from their home equity. To avoid overleveraging or loan default, it is critical to carefully consider the conditions and dangers involved with a HELOC, as well as to use the funds properly.

WHAT IS A LEASE OPTION IN REAL ESTATE, AND HOW DOES IT WORK?

A lease option, also known as a rent-to-own or lease-purchase agreement, is a contract between a landlord (seller) and a tenant (buyer) that allows the tenant to rent a property for a set amount of time with the option to buy it later. This is how a lease option works.

Agreement Terms: The lease option agreement includes the lease's terms and conditions, such as the monthly rent amount, lease term length, property purchase price, and option fee or compensation paid by the renter for the right to acquire the property.

Option Period: The lease option agreement usually includes an option period during which the tenant has the only right to buy the property at the agreed-upon price. The option period might extend from a few months to several years, depending on the terms of the agreement.

Option Fee: The tenant often pays the landlord an option fee or consideration up front in exchange for the right to purchase the property at a later date. The option fee is often non-refundable and may be applied to the purchase price of the property if the tenant exercises their option to buy.

Rent Credits: Under some lease option agreements, a percentage of the monthly rent payments may be applied to the purchase price of the property if the tenant exercises their option to buy. Rent credits encourage the tenant to follow the terms of the lease and eventually purchase the property.

Purchase Price: The lease option agreement defines the property's purchase price, which is normally calculated at the start of the lease period or based on the property's current market value when the option is exercised.

Maintenance and Repairs: The lease option agreement may include the tenant and landlord's responsibilities for maintenance and repairs during the lease term. In some circumstances, the tenant may be expected to maintain the property as if they were the owner, although the landlord is still responsible for major repairs and structural issues.

Exercise of Option: At the end of the option period, the tenant may exercise their right to acquire the property under the terms of the agreement. If the tenant does not exercise their option, they may forfeit the option money and any rent credits earned throughout the lease term.

finance: If the renter chooses to exercise their option to buy the property, they must obtain finance to complete the transaction. The terms and conditions of the financing may differ depending on the tenant's creditworthiness and the lender's criteria.

Lease options can be an advantageous arrangement for both landlords and tenants, allowing tenants to rent with the option to buy while providing landlords with potential revenue and a future buyer for their property. However, both parties must carefully analyze the provisions of the lease option agreement and weigh the potential risks and rewards before engaging into the arrangement.

WHAT IS PRIVATE MORTGAGE INSURANCE (PMI), AND WHEN IS IT REQUIRED?

Private Mortgage Insurance (PMI) is a sort of insurance that covers the lender in the event that the borrower defaults on their mortgage loan. PMI is usually required for traditional mortgages with a down payment of less than 20%. Here's how PMI works and when it's needed:

Down Payment Requirement: PMI is often required when the borrower contributes less than 20% of the home's buying price. Borrowers with a down payment of less than 20% are viewed as higher risk by lenders due to the lack of equity in the property.

The cost of PMI fluctuates according to the loan amount, loan-to-value ratio, and borrower credit score. PMI premiums are often included in the borrower's monthly mortgage payment or paid in full at closing.

Cancellation of PMI: Borrowers can request PMI cancellation if they have accumulated sufficient equity in the property, which normally occurs when the loan-to-value ratio is 80% or below.

Lenders are obligated to immediately discontinue PMI when the loan-to-value ratio exceeds 78% of the original property value.

PMI vs. FHA Mortgage Insurance: Unlike conventional mortgage loans, FHA (Federal Housing Administration) loans require borrowers to pay mortgage insurance payments (MIP) regardless of their down payment size. FHA loans may be a realistic alternative for applicants with low credit scores or a modest down payment, but they are sometimes associated with higher upfront and recurring mortgage insurance expenses.

Borrower Protections: The Homeowners Protection Act (HPA) protects borrowers with PMI, including disclosure requirements, the opportunity to request PMI cancellation, and standards for automatic PMI termination.

Impact on Affordability: PMI raises the overall cost of homeownership for borrowers by adding an extra fee to the monthly mortgage payment. Borrowers should include the expense of PMI in their budget when determining how much home they can buy.

PMI can be a useful tool for borrowers who cannot afford a 20% down payment yet want to buy a home. However, borrowers must understand the costs and implications of PMI and consider options for reducing or eliminating PMI, such as making a higher down payment or refinancing the mortgage loan.

WHAT IS A 1031 EXCHANGE IN REAL ESTATE INVESTING?

A 1031 exchange, also known as a like-kind exchange or tax-deferred exchange, is a tax strategy that real estate investors employ to defer capital gains taxes on the sale of investment property. This is how a 1031 exchange works.

A 1031 exchange allows a property owner to sell an investment property and reinvest the earnings in another like-kind property while avoiding capital gains taxes on the sale. The term "1031 exchange" relates to Section 1031 of the Internal Revenue Code, which specifies the rules and procedures for such transactions.

Like-Kind Property: To be eligible for a 1031 exchange, both the relinquished property (property being sold) and the replacement property (property being acquired) must be held for investment or commercial purposes and be of the same kind. The term "like-kind" refers to the nature or character of the investment, not the type of property (e.g., residential or commercial).

Identification Period: After selling the relinquished property, the investor has 45 days to find suitable replacement properties that meet the like-kind criteria. The identity must be in written and delivered to the qualified intermediary (QI) or escrow agent managing the transaction.

Exchange Period: The investor must execute the exchange and purchase the replacement property within 180 days of selling the relinquished property. The exchange must be carried out through a qualified intermediary (QI), who holds the profits of the sale of the relinquished property and facilitates the acquisition of the replacement property.

Tax Deferral: By executing a 1031 exchange, the investor can postpone paying capital gains taxes on the sale of the relinquished property until a later date when the replacement property is sold without undergoing another 1031 exchange. The tax liability is effectively carried over to the replacement property.

Potential Benefits: 1031 exchanges can help real estate investors defer taxes, diversify their investment portfolios, increase cash flow through property upgrades or improvements, and consolidate or exchange properties for better investment opportunities.

Complexity and standards: The IRS has established severe rules and standards for 1031 exchanges, and failure to comply with these rules can result in disqualification and immediate tax penalty. To negotiate the complexity of a 1031 exchange, investors should seek guidance from experienced specialists such as qualified intermediaries, tax advisors, and real estate attorneys.

Limitations: While 1031 exchanges provide considerable tax advantages to real estate investors, they are not appropriate for all investment scenarios. Before seeking a 1031 exchange, investors should think carefully about their investing objectives, financial circumstances, and long-term strategy.

Overall, a 1031 exchange can be an effective tax strategy for real estate owners seeking to defer capital gains taxes while increasing the return on their investment properties. However, investors must understand the laws and procedures of a 1031 exchange and obtain professional advice to ensure compliance with IRS regulations.

WHAT IS A REVERSE MORTGAGE, AND HOW DOES IT WORK?

A reverse mortgage is a financial instrument accessible to homeowners aged 62 and up that allows them to turn a portion of their home equity into cash while maintaining ownership of the property. Here's how reverse mortgages work:

Qualifications: To be eligible for a reverse mortgage, homeowners must be at least 62 years old and have substantial equity in their principal residence. The borrower must also make the home their primary residence and continue to pay property taxes, homeowners insurance, and maintain it.

Reverse mortgages are classified into numerous forms, including FHA-insured Home Equity Conversion Mortgages (HECMs) and proprietary reverse mortgages issued by private lenders.

HECMs are the most frequent type of reverse mortgage, and they are subject to specific restrictions and limitations.

Loan Amount: The amount of money that homeowners can borrow through a reverse mortgage is determined by criteria such as the borrower's age, the appraised value of the home, current interest rates, and the kind of reverse mortgage. In general, the borrower's age and the value of their home determine how much money they can borrow.

Payment Options: Borrowers with a reverse mortgage have numerous ways to receive funds, including a lump sum payment, monthly payments, a line of credit, or a combination of these. The borrower can select the payment method that best meets their financial needs and aspirations.

No Monthly Payments: Unlike typical mortgages, borrowers do not have to make monthly payments on a reverse mortgage.

Instead, the loan sum grows over time, and interest is charged on the outstanding debt. The loan is normally returned when the borrower sells the home, moves out permanently, or dies.

Repayment: When the reverse mortgage falls due, either because the borrower has died or the home is no longer occupied as their principal residence, the debt must be returned. The borrower's heirs or estate may opt to repay the loan by selling the home, refinancing it with a standard mortgage, or paying it off with other assets.

Home Equity Impact: Because the loan sum increases over time, a reverse mortgage can diminish the homeowner's equity in the property. Borrowers, on the other hand, are protected by a non-recourse feature, which means they or their successors will never owe more than the value of the home at the time of repayment.

Counseling Requirement: Before receiving a reverse mortgage, consumers must consult with a HUD-approved housing counselor. The counseling session educates borrowers about the risks and benefits of a reverse mortgage, allowing them to make informed judgments about whether it is the best financial option for them.

Reverse mortgages can be an effective financial instrument for homeowners aged 62 and above who need cash and wish to access their home equity without selling. However, before proceeding, borrowers must first grasp the terms, fees, and hazards connected with reverse mortgages, as well as carefully examine their financial goals and circumstances.

WHAT IS A SHORT SALE IN REAL ESTATE, AND HOW DOES IT WORK?

A short sale is a real estate transaction in which the homeowner sells the property for less than the outstanding mortgage balance, with the lender's approval. Short sales are generally pursued by homeowners who are experiencing financial difficulties and can no longer afford to make their mortgage payments. This is how a short sale works.

Financial Hardship: If a homeowner is facing financial difficulties, such as job loss, divorce, medical expenditures, or an adjustable-rate mortgage that has reset to a higher interest rate, they may consider a short sale. The homeowner must show the lender that they are unable to continue making mortgage payments and are at risk of default.

Lender consent: Before listing the property as a short sale, the homeowner must receive consent from their mortgage lender(s).

The lender will evaluate the homeowner's financial status, review proof of the difficulty, and determine whether a short sale is an acceptable alternative to foreclosure.

Listing the Property: Once the lender accepts the short sale, the property is offered for sale on the open market alongside other properties. To attract potential purchasers and facilitate a transaction, the listing price is often set lower than the outstanding mortgage balance.

Acceptance of an Offer: When a buyer makes an offer on the property, it is subject to the lender's acceptance of the short sale. The homeowner and their real estate agent send the offer to the lender, along with a short sale package that includes financial documentation, a hardship letter, and a suggested settlement statement.

Negotiation with the Lender: The lender evaluates the buyer's offer and the homeowner's financial information before deciding whether to accept, reject, or counter the offer.

The negotiation process can be lengthy and complicated, as the lender must balance the possible loss from a short sale against the costs of foreclosure.

Closing the Sale: If the lender authorizes the short sale, the transaction will proceed to the closing stage, just like a typical real estate sale. The buyer completes the purchase of the property, and the profits of the sale are used to pay off the remaining mortgage balance, closing expenses, and any other liens or encumbrances on the property.

Deficiency Judgment: Following the short sale, the lender may forgive the homeowner's outstanding obligation. However, in states that allow deficiency judgments, the lender may pursue the homeowner for the deficiency—the difference between the mortgage amount owing and the property's sale price.

Short sales may be a viable alternative for homeowners who are experiencing financial difficulties and need to sell their homes but owe more on their mortgage than the property is worth. Short sales, on the other hand, are complex transactions requiring collaboration among the homeowner, their lender, buyers, and real estate specialists. Homeowners considering a short sale should obtain advice from experienced real estate agents and legal specialists familiar with the process.

WHAT ARE THE HIDDEN COSTS OF HOMEOWNERSHIP?

Oh, the delights of owning! However, before signing on the dotted line, you should be aware of the hidden costs associated with property ownership. Here's an overview of what to expect:

Property taxes vary greatly depending on where you live. Prepare to budget for annual property tax payments, which can mount up over time.

Homeowners insurance protects your investment. Premiums vary depending on region, property value, and coverage selections. Don't forget to include this in your monthly budget.

Maintenance and Repairs: Homes require regular upkeep as well as periodic repairs. Plan for expenses such as grass care, HVAC maintenance, plumbing repairs, and more. It's a good idea to set aside money for unexpected repairs.

Utilities: Do not forget about your monthly utility costs! Consider the expenses of power, water, gas, garbage removal, and any other utilities specific to your area.

HOA Fees: If you reside in a community with a homeowner's association (HOA), you will most likely pay monthly or annual fees to maintain common areas and facilities. Before purchasing a property in one of these neighborhoods, ensure that you understand the HOA's regulations and fees.

Closing costs include fees for appraisals, inspections, title insurance, and legal services that are often incurred when purchasing a home. Plan to cover these upfront expenditures in addition to your down payment.

By including these hidden expenditures into your budget and financial planning, you'll be more prepared for the obligations of homeownership and able to enjoy your new home with confidence.

WHAT ARE SOME IMPORTANT CONSIDERATIONS WHEN INVESTING IN RENTAL PROPERTIES?

Investing in rental properties can be a profitable enterprise, since it provides passive income, tax breaks, and potential long-term growth. Here are some important factors to consider while investing in rental properties:

Location is one of the most important considerations when investing in rental properties. Look for properties in popular neighborhoods that have high rental demand, low vacancy rates, and room for future expansion. Consider the vicinity of facilities such as schools, parks, retail malls, and public transportation.

Property Type: Choose whether to invest in residential or commercial rental properties, single-family homes, multi-family units, condominiums, or apartment buildings. Each form of property has advantages and disadvantages in terms of rental revenue, management obligations, and appreciation potential.

Financial Analysis: Conduct a detailed financial analysis of possible rental properties to determine their income potential, expenses, cash flow, and ROI. Consider the following factors: rental income, operating expenses, property taxes, insurance, maintenance costs, vacancy rates, and financing terms.

Market Trends: Look at local market trends and economic indicators to find places with high rental demand and suitable rental market circumstances. Pay attention to things like job growth, population growth, unemployment rates, and median household income.

Property Condition: Assess the property's condition and any repairs, renovations, or improvements required to make it rentable. Consider hiring a professional home inspector to look for any hidden flaws or structural problems that could influence the property's value or rental income.

Tenant Screening: Create a rigorous tenant screening procedure to identify dependable and responsible tenants who will pay rent on time, maintain the property, and follow the conditions of the lease agreement. Conduct background checks, credit checks, and rental history verifications to determine the appropriateness of prospective tenants.

Property Management: Choose whether to manage the rental property yourself or employ a professional property management business to handle day-to-day operations such as tenant communications, maintenance requests, rent collecting, and lease enforcement. Property management costs are normally a proportion of rental income, but they can save time and effort for busy investors.

Legal and Regulatory Compliance: Become familiar with landlord-tenant legislation, fair housing regulations, and local rental regulations in the area where you intend to invest. To avoid legal concerns or tenant disputes, ensure that your lease agreements, rental rules, and property management methods are in accordance with all applicable laws and regulations.

Risk Management: Consider the hazards of investing in rental properties, such as property damage, liability claims, rental defaults, economic downturns, and unanticipated expenses. Consider getting landlord insurance, umbrella insurance, and setting aside funds for upkeep and repairs to reduce potential dangers.

Long-Term Strategy: Create a long-term investing strategy based on your financial objectives, risk tolerance, and investment time frame. Consider capital appreciation, rental income growth, tax benefits, and eventual sale or refinance strategies.

Investing in rental homes can be a profitable method to accumulate wealth and earn passive income over time. By carefully evaluating these critical aspects and completing extensive due diligence, investors may make more educated decisions and optimize the potential profits on their rental property investments.

WHAT ARE SOME TIPS FOR NEGOTIATING A HOME PURCHASE PRICE?

Negotiating the purchase price of a home is an important component of the homebuying process and can significantly affect the entire cost of the property. Here are some strategies for negotiating a home's purchasing price:

Do Your Research: Look at comparable houses in the neighborhood to obtain an idea of the market worth and current sales prices for similar homes. Consider criteria including location, size, condition, amenities, and recent renovations or upgrades.

Know Your Budget: Figure out how much you can afford to spend on a property, including the down payment, closing charges, and monthly mortgage payments. Get pre-approved for a mortgage to demonstrate your financial stability and bargaining power as a buyer.

Identify Your Priorities: Consider your home's location, size, layout, amenities, and potential for future appreciation. To stay inside your budget, be willing to sacrifice on certain features or perks.

Understand the Seller's purpose: Determine the seller's purpose for selling the home, which could be relocation, downsizing, financial trouble, or an expired listing. This information can help you modify your negotiation strategy to meet the seller's demands and interests.

Make a Competitive Offer: Base your offer on the property's market value, your budget, and the seller's asking price. Include a pre-approval letter from your lender to verify your financial stability and seriousness as a purchaser.

Negotiate Strategically: When negotiating the purchase price, consider market circumstances, the property's time on the market, and any competing offers. Prepare to negotiate pricing, closing expenses, repairs, contingencies, and other sale parameters in order to reach a mutually agreeable agreement.

Request Inspections: Schedule a home inspection to uncover any potential flaws or defects that may affect the property's value or necessitate repairs. Use the inspection report as leverage in negotiations to request repairs, credits, or a lower purchase price.

Stay Flexible: Be willing to compromise and negotiate in good faith to reach a mutually advantageous deal with the seller. Avoid making unrealistic demands or ultimatums that could jeopardize the negotiation process or spoil your connection with the seller.

Consider hiring a skilled real estate agent who has experience negotiating house purchase pricing and can give expert advice and counsel during the negotiation process. An agent can assist you in navigating complex discussions, managing paperwork, and advocating for your interests as a buyer.

Be Patient and Persistent: Negotiating a home purchase price can take time, with numerous rounds of bids and counteroffers.

Maintain patience, persistence, and positivity during the negotiation process, and be prepared to walk away if the sale terms are not beneficial or realistic for you as a buyer.

By following these guidelines and approaching the negotiation process with preparation, strategy, and flexibility, you can improve your chances of successfully negotiating a good purchase price for your ideal property. Remember to be informed, communicate effectively, and work toward a win-win situation for both you and the seller.

CONCLUSION

To summarize, navigating the world of real estate can be both thrilling and intimidating, particularly for first-time purchasers who face a slew of options and considerations. "The Ultimate Real Estate Q&A: 50 Questions Every Homebuyer MUST Ask" strives to provide vital insights and information to homebuyers, empowering them to make informed decisions along their journey.

From comprehending the nuances of mortgage alternatives to negotiating the complexity of real estate transactions, this book addresses vital issues in a conversational and approachable style. By digging into topics such as home financing, property inspections, negotiation methods, and more, readers obtain a thorough awareness of the real estate environment and feel prepared to face the homebuying process with confidence.

Each question acts as a stepping stone, bringing readers through the complexities of real estate transactions while providing useful guidance, real-world examples, and actionable solutions. Whether you're a first-time homeowner or a seasoned investor, this book will help you navigate the complexities of the real estate market with ease.

As you reach the final page, remember that knowledge is your most potent tool in the real estate industry. With the knowledge gained from "The Ultimate Real Estate Q&A," you'll be better equipped to embark on your homebuying journey with confidence, clarity, and joy. Happy house searching!

ACKNOWLEDGMENT

Writing "The Ultimate Real Estate Q&A: 50 Questions Every Homebuyer Must Ask" has been an extremely satisfying experience, and I am grateful to everyone who has helped make this book a reality.

First and foremost, I'd like to convey my heartfelt gratitude to the readers who encouraged me to establish this resource. Your inquisitiveness, enthusiasm, and passion for real estate have inspired me to delve deeply into the complexities of the homebuying process and simplify complicated concepts into straightforward, concise responses.

I'm grateful to my family and friends for their constant support and encouragement throughout the writing process. Your conviction in me has been a constant source of motivation, and I appreciate your patience, understanding, and encouraging comments during late evenings and early mornings at my computer.

I'd also like to express my heartfelt gratitude to the real estate specialists, mortgage experts, and legal advisors who kindly contributed their knowledge, insights, and expertise. Your advice has been crucial in refining the content of this book, assuring its correctness and usefulness to readers.

A special thanks to the publishing house team for their hard work, professionalism, and attention to detail in bringing this book to reality. Your enthusiasm for high-quality literature and dedication to perfection have helped make my idea a reality.

Last but not least, I'd like to convey my heartfelt gratitude to the innumerable individuals that work tirelessly behind the scenes to keep the real estate sector thriving. From real estate agents and mortgage brokers to house inspectors and title officers, your hard work, devotion, and professionalism form the foundation of the housing industry.

I want to express my heartfelt gratitude to everyone who helped make "The Ultimate Real Estate Q&A" a reality. May this book be a great resource and guide for homebuyers everywhere as they begin their journey to homeownership.

With genuine appreciation,

The Ultimate Real Estate Q&A: 65 Questions Every Homebuyer MUST Ask

www.ingramcontent.com/pod-product-compliance
Lightning Source LLC
Chambersburg PA
CBHW071053240526
45471CB00015B/1801